40
Fabulous
Afghans

40 Fabulous Afghans

by Patricia Bevans

Meredith® Press

New York

We Care!
All of us at Meredith® Books are dedicated to offering you quality craft books. We welcome your comments and suggestions. Please address your correspondence to: Customer Service Department, Meredith® Press, Meredith Corporation, 150 East 52nd Street, New York, NY 10022, or call 1-800-678-2665.

Meredith® Press is an imprint of Meredith® Books:
President, Book Group: Joseph J. Ward
Vice President, Editorial Director: Elizabeth P. Rice

For Meredith® Press:
Executive Editor: Connie Schrader
Project Manager: Marsha Jahns
Editorial Assistant: Carolyn Mitchell
Production Manager: Bill Rose
Copy Editing and Proof: Sydne Matus
Book Design: Diane Wagner
Photography: Schecter Lee
Photo Styling: Dina von Zweck
Illustrations: Gary Tong
Credits:
Bed linens (pages 111, 141, and 127), Esprit Bath & Bed from West Point Pepperell Consumer Products Division; bed linens (pages 25, 33, 39, 42, 51, 69, 79, 88, 113, and 139); Wamsutta®/Pacific® Home Products; bag and engagement/address book (page 91), Coach Leather.

Toy collection courtesy of Adam Diamond.

Special thanks to Nan and Don Mitchell, who generously provided us with their house and grounds for photography . . . and remained gracious throughout long days of the photo shoot.

ISBN: 0-696-02357-1
Library of Congress Catalog Card Number: 91-052558

Printed in the United States of America
10 9 8 7 6 5 4 3 2 1

Dear Crocheter:

Are any crochet projects welcomed with more enthusiasm by crafters than afghans? In *40 Fabulous Afghans* we present an exciting array of crocheted afghans that is sure to delight beginning, intermediate, and experienced crafters alike. Whatever your preference—contemporary or classic patterns, city or country style, soft pastels or bright, primary colors—you'll find plenty of afghans to choose from. We've even included a special chapter on children's afghans.

Each project features a color photograph and detailed, step-by-step instructions, a hallmark of Meredith® Press crafts books. Look for others in your Better Homes and Gardens® Crafts Club catalog or local bookstore.

As you leaf through the pages of *40 Fabulous Afghans*, we're certain you'll find ideas and inspiration you can put to use from season to season, year after year. Enjoy!

Cordially,

Marsha Jahns

Dedication

To everyone who enjoys needlework, and most especially
to the countless crafters who so willingly and
patiently share their expertise with others.

Acknowledgment

I would like to thank my friends Dale Christensen
and Jane Miner for kindly making the
Colonial Star and Ticking Stripe afghans for me.

Contents

INTRODUCTION

Afghans have been a perennial favorite with crafters for ever so many reasons.

An afghan is cozy to cuddle under on a snowy afternoon, or an oh-so-welcome extra coverlet to chase the chill from a dark winter's night.

But in addition to providing warmth, afghans also have many decorating possibilities. Draped over a sofa or folded at the foot of a bed, an afghan serves as a decorative accent.

An afghan can complement the decor, unify a room's color scheme, or be the focal point of a decorating plan. It can even be used for seasonal effect, heralding the arrival of a new season or helping to set the mood for a special holiday.

This book includes a splendid array of afghans, in a full palette of colors and a wide range of styles. There are quilt-inspired afghans, charming country coverlets, sophisticated geometric designs, winsome child-size blankets, and afghans that capture the romance of faraway lands and long-ago times.

All of the afghans are fun and easy to do, and most can be made by beginning or intermediate crocheters. A number of the afghans are in the quick-to-complete category, but all of them can be finished in a reasonable amount of time. Many of the afghans are portable projects, for you to bring along wherever your busy life takes you.

Complete, detailed instructions and diagrams are included for each afghan. Additional information helpful for completing the projects is included in the illustrated reference chapter entitled "Crochet Stitches and Techniques."

The afghans have been designed with you in mind—no matter what your personal style is, you'll be sure to find many projects that inspire you to create an object of beauty for your own home or to give as a very special gift!

Patricia Bevans

Getting Started

Tools and Materials

To begin, in addition to crochet hooks and yarn, you'll need:

   a small ruler for measuring gauge;
   a tape measure for measuring the work;
   a pair of scissors for cutting the yarn;
   stainless steel pins to join sections for seaming;
   a blunt-ended, large-eyed needle (such as a tapestry or yarn needle) for sewing pieces together.

HOOKS

Plastic and aluminum crochet hooks are available in sizes 1/B to 10½/K, with B being the smallest and K the largest. The hooks are approximately 5″ long and have a slight contour at the hook end.

Smaller hooks are appropriate for lighter-weight yarns, larger hooks for heavier-weight yarns.

Hook sizes are specified for each pattern. Since stitch tension varies among crocheters (some work loosely, others tightly), the hook size specified should be used as a guide only. The hook size that gives you the gauge specified in the pattern should be used.

A U.S. to English and Continental hook size conversion chart is included for convenience.

YARN

Yarn is categorized by fiber content, by weight, and by texture.

There are natural fibers such as wool and cotton, and man-made fibers such as acrylic and nylon. The term *blend* is used when several types of fiber are combined in the same yarn.

Natural fibers are thought to be softer and more durable than man-made fibers, but they are often more expensive and require more care. Man-made fibers are constantly being improved, and many are not only soft and durable but have the added advantage of being reasonably priced and easy to care for. Blends of natural and man-made fibers can have the advantages of both. Information on fiber content and care requirements is included on the yarn label.

The weight of a yarn refers to the thickness to which a fiber is spun. The thickness of a yarn determines the gauge (or number of stitches per inch) to which it can be worked. Sport, worsted, and chunky are common weights. Weight information is often provided on the label in the form of a recommended knitting gauge. Sport-weight yarn has a recommended gauge of 5½ to 6 stitches per inch, worsted-weight a recommended gauge of 4 to 5 stitches per inch, and chunky-weight a recommended gauge of fewer than 4 stitches per inch. Crocheters can use recommended knitting gauge information to determine the weight of the yarn, but should not expect to get the same number of stitches per inch. Generally, crochet has fewer stitches per inch than knitting.

The texture of a yarn influences the look of the finished project. It can be smooth, brushed, crinkled, or bumpy. Smooth yarns emphasize the stitch most clearly, brushed yarns soften it, and crinkled or bumpy yarns obscure it.

CROCHET HOOKS (ALUMINUM OR PLASTIC)

U.S.	1/B	2/C	3/D	4/E	5/F	6/G	8/H	9/I	10/J	10½/K
English	12	11	10	9	8	7	6	5	4	2
Continental—mm	2.25	2.75	3.25	3.5	3.75	4.25	5	5.5	6	6.5

The yarns specified in the instructions should be used to duplicate the projects in this book. However, an attractive, similar afghan can be made with another yarn if some simple guidelines are followed. Always substitute a yarn with the same fiber content, weight, and texture as the one specified. Be sure to make a test swatch and adjust the hook size until the gauge specified in the pattern is obtained.

Yarn is sold in balls or skeins. The weight in ounces and/or grams (3½ ounces equals 100 grams; 1¾ ounces equals 50 grams) and the yardage per ball are stated on the label. Yardage is the more significant measurement and this can vary widely from one yarn to another. When making substitutions, determine your quantity requirements by yardage so that you'll be sure to have enough yarn to complete the project.

When you are starting, always buy enough yarn to complete the project. Yarn is dyed in lots, which are indicated by a number on the label. There can be subtle variations in shade between different dye lots, which will show on a finished afghan. Be sure to purchase all your balls of yarn from the same dye lot.

Easily obtainable, reasonably priced sport-, worsted-, and chunky-weight yarns were used for the projects in the book.

Understanding Crochet Patterns

Crochet patterns use standard abbreviations. A list of these abbreviations follows.

Crochet Abbreviations

bpdc	back post double crochet
CC	contrast color
ch(s)	chain(s)
ch sp	chain space
dc	double crochet
dec	decrease
fpdc	front post double crochet
hdc	half double crochet
inc	increase
lp(s)	loop(s)
MC	main color
oz	ounce(s)
rnd(s)	round(s)
sc	single crochet
sk	skip
sl st	slip stitch
sp(s)	space(s)
st(s)	stitch(es)
tog	together
tr	triple crochet
yd	yards
yo	wrap yarn over hook
"	inches
*	repeat instructions from or between asterisk(s) across or as many times as directed
()	repeat instructions within parentheses as many times as directed
[]	repeat instructions within brackets as many times as directed

The patterns have been graded according to the degree of skill required to complete them: Beginner, Intermediate, and Experienced. If you've never crocheted before, don't despair. Refer to the chapter entitled "Crochet Stitches and Techniques" for information and help. With a little practice you'll soon be comfortable enough with the basics to start a beginner afghan. Remember that even the most proficient crocheters started out as beginners!

GAUGE

Gauge is the term used to indicate the number of stitches and rows per inch of fabric. Working to the gauge stated in a pattern will yield a project of the size specified. To test the gauge, work at least a 4″ × 4″ swatch. Dividing the number of stitches by the measurement of the swatch (in inches) gives the gauge per inch. If you have **more** stitches per inch than the pattern specifies, try a larger hook; if you have **fewer** stitches, try a smaller hook. Keep adjusting the hook size until you obtain the specified gauge. Even a small difference in gauge affects the size of the project. For example, a pattern might specify a gauge of 4 stitches per inch for an afghan with a finished width of 38″. If the pattern is worked at a gauge of 4½ stitches per inch, the afghan will have a finished width of 34″— a difference of 4″. If the same pattern were worked at a gauge of 3½ stitches per inch, the finished width would be 43″. Either might be unacceptable.

Check the measurement of the piece as you go to be sure that you are keeping to gauge. Make horizontal measurements from edge to edge, being sure that the tape measure runs straight across and is not tilted at an angle. Make vertical measurements from top to bottom, again being sure that the tape measure is not tilted at an angle.

WORKING FROM CHARTS

Crochet can often be worked from a chart. Charting designs avoids lengthy explanations and enables the crafter to see at a glance how to proceed. Many crocheters find this method of working a design easier.

Each block on a chart represents 1 stitch and row. If a design is symmetrical, the chart can be read from right to left for every row. If, however, a design is asymmetrical, right-side rows are read from right to left, and wrong-side rows are read from left to right. The instructions for a project will indicate when the latter method of chart reading must be used.

When charts are used for color work, each block represents 1 stitch and row in the stitch being used for the project. The color of each stitch to be worked is indicated by the color code provided with the chart.

Charts can also be used for texture patterns. When charts are used in this way, each block still represents 1 stitch and row, but the type of stitch to be worked varies from block to block and from row to row. The type of stitch to use is indicated on the chart by the International Crochet Symbol for that stitch. A table of International Crochet Symbols follows.

International Crochet Symbols

o   chain stitch

<   slip stitch

+   single crochet

T   half double crochet

∓   double crochet

∓   triple crochet

Country Style

Crazy Quilt
Intermediate

*Add spice to country decor with a crocheted
version of a quilt favorite!
Granny squares, in a variety of colors and arrangements,
are used in this portable project.*

SIZE
42″ × 66″

MATERIALS
Phildar Leader (worsted-weight acrylic), 3½ oz/216 yd
balls: 9 balls Navy (MC); 2 balls Turquoise (A); 3
balls Red (B); 2 balls Yellow (C)
Size H/8 crochet hook (or size for gauge)

GAUGE
Each 4-round square = 4″

SEE
Reverse Slip Stitch and Working in Rounds

NOTE
Joining slip stitch counts as last chain of round.

THE AFGHAN

SECTION 1 (make 12)
With A, ch 4; join with sl st to form ring.
Rnd 1 (right side): Ch 3 (first dc), 2 dc in ring, (ch
2, 3 dc in ring) 3 times, ch 1; join with sl st to top of
ch-3; end.
Rnd 2: With right side facing, join B in any corner
sp; ch 3 (first dc), **don't** turn, 2 dc in sp, ch 2, 3 dc
in same sp, (ch 1, 3 dc in next sp, ch 2, 3 dc in same
sp) 3 times; join with sl st to top of ch-3; end.

Rnd 3: With right side facing, join C in any corner
sp; ch 3 (first dc), **don't** turn, 2 dc in sp, ch 2, 3 dc
in same sp, ch 1, 3 dc in next sp, (ch 1, 3 dc in next
sp, ch 2, 3 dc in same sp, ch 1, 3 dc in next sp) 3
times; join with sl st to top of ch-3; end.
Rnd 4: With MC, work as for Rnd 3, making 1 more
3-dc group per side; end.

SECTION 2 (make 12)
Work as for Section 1 **but** use C for Rnd 1, B for Rnd
2, A for Rnd 3, and MC for Rnd 4.

SECTION 3 (make 8)
Work as for Section 1 **but** use MC for Rnd 1, A for
Rnd 2, B for Rnd 3, and MC for Rnd 4.

SECTION 4 (make 4)
Work as for Section 1 **but** use A for Rnd 1 and MC
for Rnds 2, 3, and 4.

SECTION 5 (make 8)
Work as for Section 4 **but** use B for Rnd 1.

SECTION 6 (make 4)
Work as for Section 4 **but** use C for Rnd 1.

SECTION 7 (make 8)

Working as for Section 1, make four 2-rnd squares using A for Rnd 1 and MC for Rnd 2. To make section, with right sides facing, MC, and sl st, catching outer lps only, crochet squares together to form two 2-square rows.

SECTION 8 (make 8)

Work as for Section 7 **but** use B for Rnd 1.

SECTION 9 (make 8)

Work as for Section 7 **but** use C for Rnd 1.

SECTION 10 (make 4)

Working as for Section 1, make three 2-rnd squares using B for Rnd 1 and MC for Rnd 2. To make section, crochet squares together, in same manner as for Section 7, to form a single strip. Work edging to complete section.

Edging

With right side facing, join MC in any corner sp.

Rnd 1: Ch 3 (first dc), 2 dc in sp, ch 2, 3 dc in same sp, (ch 1, 3 dc), repeat between () into each sp and joining to corner, *ch 1, 3 dc in corner sp, ch 2, 3 dc in same sp, repeat between () into each sp and joining to corner, repeat from * 2 times more; join with sl st to top of ch-3.

Rnd 2: Sl st to corner sp, ch 3 (first dc), **don't** turn, 2 dc in sp, ch 2, 3 dc in same sp, (ch 1, 3 dc in next sp), repeat between () to corner, *ch 1, 3 dc in corner sp, ch 2, 3 dc in same sp, repeat between () to corner, repeat from * 2 times more; join with sl st to top of ch-3; end.

SECTION 11 (make 4)

Work as for Section 10 **but** use C for Rnd 1 of square.

SECTION 12 (make 4)

Work as for Section 10 **but** for square use MC for Rnd 1 and A for Rnd 2. For edging use A for Rnd 1 and MC for Rnd 2.

SECTION 13 (make 8)

Work as for Section 12 **but** use B for Rnd 1 of edging.

SECTION 14 (make 8)

Work as for Section 10 **but** for square use MC for Rnd 1 and C for Rnd 2. For edging use B for Rnd 1 and MC for Rnd 2.

SECTION 15 (make 8)

Work as for Section 10 **but** for square use C for Rnd 1 and B for Rnd 2. For edging use B for Rnd 1 and MC for Rnd 2.

SECTION 16 (make 8)

Work as for Section 15 **but** use B where C is called for and C where B is called for.

ASSEMBLY

Refer to Assembly Diagram. The diagram represents one quarter of the afghan. Following diagram, crochet small sections together, in same manner as for squares, to form a quarter segment. Repeat 3 times more.

Crochet 2 quarter segments together, joining side B of first piece to side A of second piece. Repeat 1 time more. Then, join side D of first 2 pieces to side C of second 2 pieces.

EDGING

With right side facing, join MC in any corner sp.

Rnds 1–2: Work Rnds 1–2 of Section 10 Edging around entire outer edge of afghan; **don't** end.

Rnd 3: Ch 1, **don't** turn, sc in each st and sp around, making 3 sc in each corner sp; join with sl st to first sc; **don't** end.

Rnd 4: Ch 1, **don't** turn, work a reverse sl st in each st of previous rnd; join with sl st to first reverse sl st; end.

Secure and trim loose ends.

CRAZY QUILT ASSEMBLY DIAGRAM
(One Quarter of Afghan)

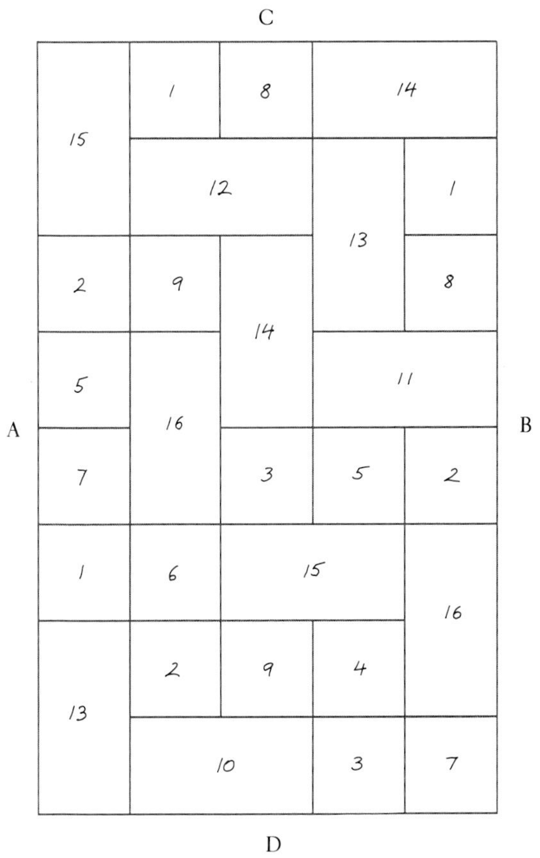

19

Apple Time

Intermediate

*At harvest time, apples shine with ruby-red ripeness
against a background of mature green leaves.
Single crochet, cross-stitch embroidery,
and weaving are used in this portable project.*

SIZE
42″ × 58½″

MATERIALS
Phildar Leader (worsted-weight acrylic), 3½ oz/216 yd
   balls: 5 balls Green (A); 7 balls White (B); 1 ball
   Red (C)
Size K/10½ crochet hook (or size for gauge)
Yarn needle

GAUGE
Each square = 8¼″

SEE
Cross-stitch Embroidery, Reverse Slip Stitch, Surface
Slip Stitch, and Weaving

THE AFGHAN

BASIC SQUARE
Ch 31.
Row 1: Sc in 2nd ch from hook and each ch across—
30 sts.
Rows 2–37: Ch 1, turn, sc in first st and each st across;
end.

SQUARE 1
Make **14** squares with A.

SQUARE 2
Make 9 squares with B. Work embroidery to complete
square.

Embroidery
The design is worked in cross-stitch embroidery. Use
the yarn needle and a single strand of yarn. **Refer to
Embroidery Chart.** Embroider following chart.

SQUARE 3
Make **12** squares with B. Work weaving to complete
square.

Weaving
Cut 70″ lengths of A. Use the yarn needle and a single
strand of yarn for each group of plaid lines. It is important that weaving be neither too tight nor too loose,
and that a sufficient length of yarn be left at **each** end
to secure later.
Refer to Weaving Chart. Begin the first vertical
plaid line as follows: Count over 7 sts from **your** right,
bring needle to front of work through space **between**
7th and 8th sts horizontally and **below** Row 1 verti-
cally. Draw yarn through space. Insert needle into
space above space just worked and draw yarn through
to back of work. Bring needle to front of work through
space above space just worked. Continue in same manner to top edge.

APPLE TIME EMBROIDERY CHART

APPLE TIME WEAVING CHART

Each block = 1 stitch and row
(count turning ch as 1 st when embroidering)
∘ = A
x = C

Each block = Space between stitch and row
(count turning ch as 1 st when weaving)
∘ = Space into which weaving is worked

22

Turn work so top edge is closest to you and work next vertical line as for first, into spaces to right of spaces just worked (between 8th and 9th sts).

Following chart, complete remaining vertical plaid lines in same manner.

Work horizontal plaid lines as for vertical lines, starting at edge to your right and working around posts of sts into spaces between rows.

ASSEMBLY
Refer to Assembly Diagram. With right sides facing, corresponding color, and overcast st, sew squares together following diagram.

EDGING
With right side facing, join A.

Rnd 1: Work a rnd of sc evenly around entire piece, making 3 sc at each corner; join with sl st to first sc.

Rnd 2: Ch 1, **don't** turn, work a reverse sl st in each st of previous rnd; join with sl st to first reverse sl st.

Rnd 3: Ch 1, **don't** turn, working below previous rnd, work a rnd of surface sl st around posts of sts of Rnd 1; join with sl st to first surface sl st; end.

Secure and trim loose ends.

APPLE TIME ASSEMBLY DIAGRAM

2	3	1	3	2
3	1	2	1	3
1	3	1	3	1
2	1	2	1	2
1	3	1	3	1
3	1	2	1	3
2	3	1	3	2

Log Cabin

Intermediate

An ever popular quilt pattern makes a charming accent for a country room. A variation of the granny square is used in this portable project.

SIZE
52½" × 68½"

MATERIALS
Phildar Leader (worsted-weight acrylic), 3½ oz/216 yd balls: 4 balls Aqua (A); 1 ball White (B); 2 balls each Royal Blue (C), Baby Blue (D), and Turquoise (E); 6 balls Navy (F)
Size H/8 crochet hook (or size for gauge)

GAUGE
Each square = 8⅛"

SEE
Reverse Slip Stitch and Working in Rounds

NOTE
Joining slip stitch counts as last chain of round.

THE AFGHAN

SQUARE (make 48)
Refer to Square Diagram. Follow the directions below for each part of the basic square.

Center
With A, ch 4; join with sl st to form ring.
Rnd 1 (right side): Ch 3 (first dc), 2 dc in ring, (ch 2, 3 dc in ring) 3 times, ch 1; join with sl st to top of ch-3.
Rnd 2: Ch 3 (first dc), **turn,** 2 dc in sp, ch 2, 3 dc in same sp, (ch 1, 3 dc in next sp, ch 2, 3 dc in same sp) 3 times; join with sl st to top of ch-3; end.

Section 1
With right side facing, join B in any corner sp.
Rnd 1 (right side): Ch 4 (first dc, ch 1), 3 dc in next sp, ch 1, 3 dc in next sp, ch 2, 3 dc in same sp, ch 1, 3 dc in next sp, ch 1, dc in corner sp.
Rnd 2: Ch 3 (first dc), **turn,** 2 dc in sp, (ch 1, 3 dc in next sp) 2 times, ch 2, 3 dc in same sp, repeat between () 2 times more; end.

Section 2
With right side facing, join C to top of starting ch-3 of last rnd.
Rnd 1 (right side): Ch 4 (first dc, ch 1), 2 dc in next sp, dc in next sp, (ch 1, 3 dc in next sp) 2 times, ch

LOG CABIN SQUARE DIAGRAM

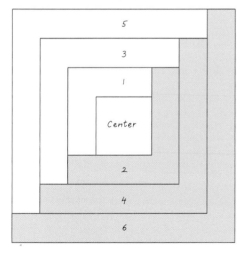

Shading indicates dark side of square.

24

2, 3 dc in same sp, repeat between () 1 time more, ch 1, dc in next sp, 2 dc in next sp, ch 1, dc in top of corner st.

Rnd 2: Ch 3 (first dc), **turn,** 2 dc in sp, (ch 1, 3 dc in next sp) 3 times, ch 2, 3 dc in same sp, repeat between () 3 times more; end.

Section 3

With right side facing, join D to top of starting ch-3 of last rnd.

Rnd 1 (right side): Ch 4 (first dc, ch 1), 3 dc in next sp, (ch 1, 3 dc in next sp) 3 times, ch 2, 3 dc in same sp, repeat between () 3 times more, ch 1, dc in top of corner st.

Rnd 2: Ch 3 (first dc), **turn,** 2 dc in sp, (ch 1, 3 dc in next sp) 4 times, ch 2, 3 dc in same sp, repeat between () 4 times more; end.

Section 4

With E, work as for Section 3, making 1 more 3-dc group per side per rnd; end.

Section 5

With A, work as for Section 3, making 2 more 3-dc groups per side per rnd; end.

Section 6

With F, work as for Section 3, making 3 more 3-dc groups per side per rnd; end.

LOG CABIN AFGHAN ASSEMBLY DIAGRAM

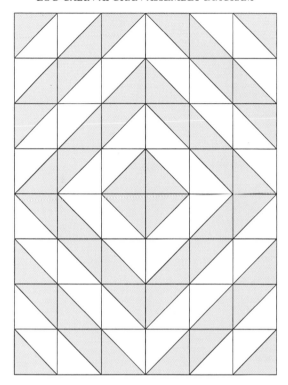

Shading indicates dark side of square.

ASSEMBLY

Refer to Afghan Assembly Diagram. Shading indicates dark side of square. With right sides facing, corresponding color, and sl st, catching outer lps only, crochet squares together to form vertical strips. Join vertical strips in same manner.

EDGING

With right side facing, join F in any corner sp.

Rnd 1: Ch 3 (first dc), 2 dc in sp, ch 2, 3 dc in same sp, (ch 1, 3 dc); repeat between () into each ch-1 sp, F-colored dc sp, and joining to corner; *ch 1, 3 dc in corner sp, ch 2, 3 dc in same sp; repeat between () into each ch-1 sp, F-colored dc sp, and joining to corner; repeat from * 2 times more; join with sl st to top of ch-3.

Rnd 2: Sl st to corner sp, 2 sl st in sp, ch 3 (first dc), **turn,** 2 dc in sp, ch 2, 3 dc in same sp, (ch 1, 3 dc in next sp), repeat between () to corner, *ch 1, 3 dc in corner sp, ch 2, 3 dc in same sp, repeat between () to corner, repeat from * 2 times more; join with sl st to top of ch-3.

Rnd 3: Ch 1, **turn,** sc in each st and sp around, making 3 sc in each corner sp; join with sl st to first sc.

Rnd 4: Ch 1, **don't** turn, work a reverse sl st in each st of previous rnd; join with sl st to first reverse sl st; end.

Secure and trim loose ends.

Diamond

Intermediate

Color it Christmas, and capture the magic year-round!
Double crochet carried-thread color work is used
in this quick-to-complete project.

SIZE
46″ × 62″

MATERIALS
Bernat Berella "4" (worsted-weight acrylic) 3½ oz/240 yd balls: 4 balls Dark Green (A); 5 balls White (B); 1 ball each Bright Green (C), Rose (D), and Red (E)

Size H/8 crochet hook (or size for gauge)

GAUGE
11 sts = 3″; 9 rows = 5″ (in pattern stitch)

SEE
Changing Color and Reverse Slip Stitch

ONE-PIECE AFGHAN
With A, ch 167.

Refer to Stitch Chart.

Row 1 (right side): Work Chart Row 1 as follows: From X *to* Y: with A, dc in 4th ch from hook, dc in next ch; (with C, dc in next 3 chs; with A, dc in next 3 chs) 13 times; with B, dc in next ch; from Y *to* Z: with B, dc in next ch; then from Y *to* X: with B, dc in next ch; with A, dc in next 3 chs; (with C, dc in next 3 chs; with A, dc in next 3 chs) 13 times—165 sts.

Row 2: Work Chart Row 2 as follows: From X *to* Y: with A, ch 3 (first dc), turn, sk first st, dc in next 2 sts; (with C, dc in next 3 sts; with A, dc in next 3 sts) 13 times; with B, dc in next st; from Y *to* Z: with B, dc in next st; then from Y *to* X: with B, dc in next st; with A, dc in next 3 sts; (with C, dc in next 3 sts; with A, dc in next 3 sts) 13 times.

Row 3: Work Chart Row 3 as follows: From X *to* Y: with D, ch 3 (first dc), turn, sk first st, dc in next 2 sts; (with A, dc in next 3 sts; with D, dc in next 3 sts) 12 times; with A, dc in next 3 sts; with B, dc in next 4 sts; from Y *to* Z: with B, dc in next st; then from Y *to* X: with B, dc in next 4 sts; with A, dc in next 3 sts; with D, dc in next 3 sts; (with A, dc in next 3 sts; with D, dc in next 3 sts) 12 times.

Row 4: Work Chart Row 4 (and all wrong-side rows) by repeating previous row.

Work Chart Rows 5–110 in same manner; end.

EDGING
With right side facing, join A.

Rnd 1: Work a rnd of sc evenly around entire piece, making 3 sc at each corner; join with sl st to first sc.

Rnd 2: Ch 2 (first hdc), **don't** turn, sk first st, hdc in each st around, making 3 hdc at each corner; join with sl st to top of ch-2.

Rnd 3: Ch 1, **don't** turn, work a reverse sl st in each st of previous rnd; join with sl st to first reverse sl st; end.

Secure and trim loose ends.

DIAMOND STITCH CHART

Row 110

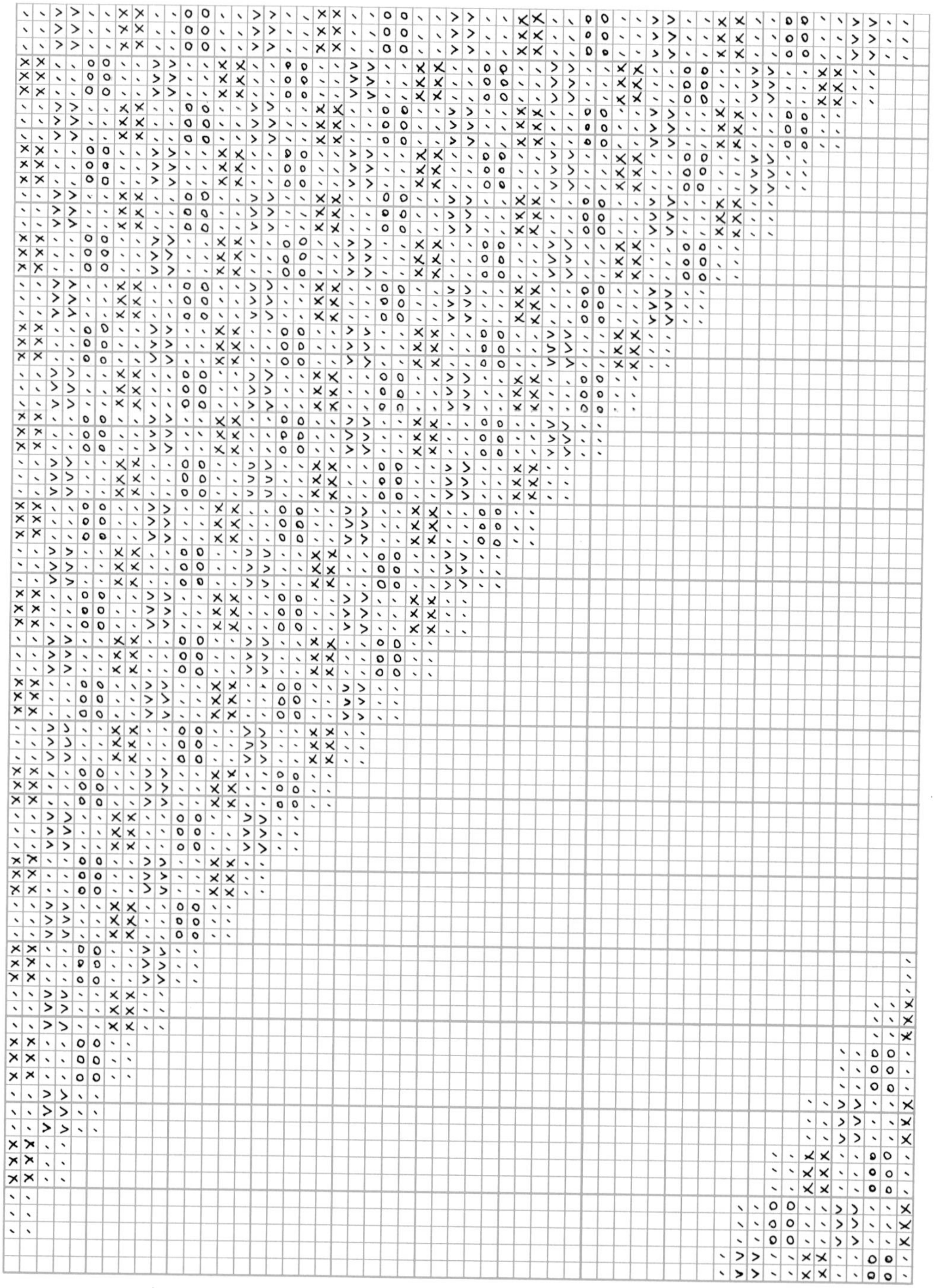

Center

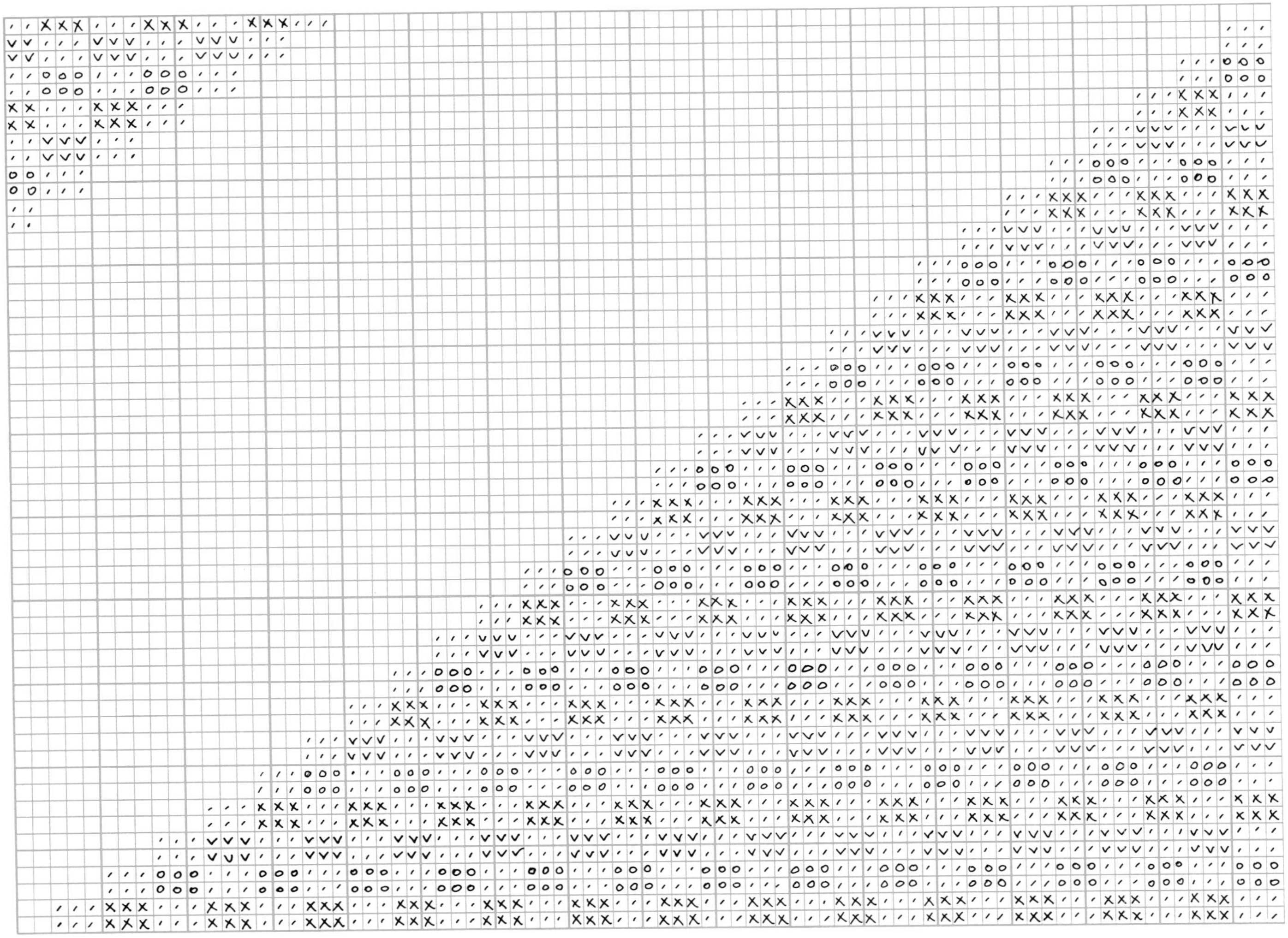

X

ZY

Center

′ = A

□ = B

× = C

o = D

v = E

Each block = 1 stitch and row

31

Patchwork Star

Intermediate

Star light, star bright, last star you'll see at night!
Basic and diagonal color-change granny squares
are used in this portable project.

SIZE
57½" × 75½"

MATERIALS
Patons Astra (sport-weight acrylic), 1¾ oz/182 yd balls:
12 balls Cream (A); 1 ball Pink (B); 2 balls Aqua
(C); 3 balls Rose (D); 10 balls Teal (E)
Size F/5 crochet hook (or size for gauge)

GAUGE
Each square = 3⅝"

SEE
Changing Color, Reverse Slip Stitch, and Working in
Rounds

NOTE
Joining slip stitch counts as last chain of round.

THE AFGHAN

SQUARE 1 (make 48)
With A, ch 4; join with sl st to form ring.

Rnd 1 (right side): Ch 3 (first dc), 2 dc in ring, (ch
2, 3 dc in ring) 3 times, ch 1; join with sl st to top of
ch-3.

Rnd 2: Ch 3 (first dc), **turn,** 2 dc in sp, ch 2, 3 dc in
same sp, (ch 1, 3 dc in next sp, ch 2, 3 dc in same
sp) 3 times; join with sl st to top of ch-3.

Rnd 3: Sl st to corner sp, 2 sl st in sp, ch 3 (first dc),
turn, 2 dc in sp, ch 2, 3 dc in same sp, ch 1, 3 dc in
next sp, (ch 1, 3 dc in next sp, ch 2, 3 dc in same sp,
ch 1, 3 dc in next sp) 3 times; join with sl st to top of
ch-3.

Rnd 4: Work as for Rnd 3, making 1 more 3-dc group
per side; end.

SQUARE 2 (make 48)
Work as for Square 1 **but** end between rnds, using
B for Rnd 1, C for Rnd 2, D for Rnd 3, and E for
Rnd 4.

SQUARE 3 (make 96)
With A, ch 4; join with sl st to form ring.

Rnd 1 (right side): Ch 3 (first dc), 2 dc in ring, ch 2,
3 dc in ring, ch 1; with **B** (don't end A), ch 1, 3 dc
in ring, ch 2, 3 dc in ring, ch 1; join with sl st to top
of ch-3; end B.

Rnd 2: Join C in corner sp just completed; ch 3 (first
dc), **turn,** 2 dc in sp, *ch 1, 3 dc in next sp, ch 2, 3
dc in same sp, ch 1, 3 dc in next sp, ch 1*; with **A,**
ch 1 (end C), 3 dc in same sp, repeat between *s; join
with sl st to top of ch-3; **don't** end.

Rnd 3: Continuing with A, ch 1, **turn,** sl st in corner
sp just completed, ch 3 (first dc), 2 dc in sp, *(ch 1,
3 dc in next sp) 2 times, ch 2, 3 dc in same sp, repeat
between () 2 times more, ch 1*; with **D** (don't end
A), ch 1, 3 dc in same sp, repeat between *s; join with
sl st to top of ch 3; end D.

Rnd 4: Join E in corner sp just completed; ch 3 (first
dc), **turn,** 2 dc in sp, *(ch 1, 3 dc in next sp) 3 times,
ch 2, 3 dc in same sp, repeat between () 3 times more,
ch 1*; with **A,** ch 1 (end E), 3 dc in same sp, repeat
between *s; join with sl to top of ch-3; end.

BLOCK ASSEMBLY

Refer to Assembly Diagram. Shading indicates multicolored areas. With right sides facing, corresponding color, and sl st, catching outer lps only, crochet squares together to form blocks.

BLOCK BORDER

With right side facing, join A in any corner sp.

Rnd 1: Ch 3 (first dc), 2 dc in sp, ch 2, 3 dc in same sp, (ch 1, 3 dc), repeat between () into each sp and joining to corner, *ch 1, 3 dc in corner sp, ch 2, 3 dc in same sp, repeat between () into each sp and joining to corner, repeat from * 2 times more; join with sl st to top of ch-3.

Rnd 2: Sl st to corner sp, 2 sl st in sp, ch 3 (first dc), **turn,** 2 dc in sp, ch 2, 3 dc in same sp, (ch 1, 3 dc in next sp), repeat between () to corner, *ch 1, 3 dc in corner sp, ch 2, 3 dc in same sp, repeat between () to corner, repeat from * 2 times more; join with sl st to top of ch-3; end.

Rnd 3: With wrong side facing, join E in any corner sp; work as for Rnd 2, beginning with ch-3; **don't** end.

Rnd 4: Continuing with E, repeat Rnd 2; end.

AFGHAN ASSEMBLY

Crochet blocks together, in same manner as for squares, to form four 3-block rows.

AFGHAN EDGING

With right side facing, join E in any corner sp.

Rnds 1–2: Work Rnds 1–2 of Block Border around entire outer edge of afghan; **don't** end.

Rnd 3: Ch 1, **turn,** sc in each st and sp around, making 3 sc in each corner sp; join with sl st to first sc.

Rnd 4: Ch 1, **don't** turn, work a reverse sl st in each st of previous rnd; join with sl st to first reverse sl st; end.

Secure and trim loose ends.

PATCHWORK STAR ASSEMBLY DIAGRAM

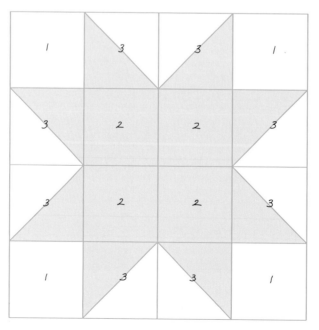

Shading indicates multicolored areas.

Windmills

Intermediate

*Beautifully blue and crisply white windmill shapes
suggest Dutch tiles. Basic and diagonal color-change
granny squares are used in this portable project.*

SIZE
48" × 66"

MATERIALS
Patons Astra (sport-weight acrylic), 1¾ oz/182 yd balls:
   10 balls Blue (MC); 8 balls White (CC)
Size F/5 crochet hook (or size for gauge)

GAUGE
Each square = 3"

SEE
Changing Color, Reverse Slip Stitch, and Working in Rounds

NOTE
Joining slip stitch counts as last chain of round.

THE AFGHAN

SQUARE A (make 72)
With MC, ch 4; join with sl st to form ring.
Rnd 1 (right side): Ch 3 (first dc), 2 dc in ring, ch 2, 3 dc in ring, ch 1; with **CC** (**don't** end MC), ch 1, 3 dc in ring, ch 2, 3 dc in ring, ch 1; join with sl st to top of ch-3; **don't** end.
Rnd 2: Continuing with CC, ch 1, **turn**, sl st in corner sp just completed, ch 3 (first dc), 2 dc in sp, *ch 1, 3 dc in next sp, ch 2, 3 dc in same sp, ch 1, 3 dc in next sp, ch 1*; with **MC**, (**don't** end CC), ch 1, 3 dc in same sp, repeat between *s; join with sl st to top of ch-3; **don't** end.
Rnd 3: Continuing with MC, ch 1, **turn**, sl st in corner sp just completed, ch 3 (first dc), 2 dc in sp, *(ch 1,
3 dc in next sp) 2 times, ch 2, 3 dc in same sp, repeat between () 2 times more, ch 1*; with **CC** (end MC), ch 1, 3 dc in same sp, repeat between *s; join with sl st to top of ch 3; end.

SQUARE B (make 32)
With MC, ch 4; join with sl st to form ring.
Rnd 1 (right side): Ch 3 (first dc), 2 dc in ring, (ch 2, 3 dc in ring) 3 times, ch 1; join with sl st to top of ch-3.
Rnd 2: Ch 3 (first dc), **turn**, 2 dc in sp, ch 2, 3 dc in same sp, (ch 1, 3 dc in next sp, ch 2, 3 dc in same sp) 3 times; join with sl st to top of ch-3.
Rnd 3: Sl st to corner sp, 2 sl st in sp, ch 3 (first dc), **turn**, 2 dc in sp, ch 2, 3 dc in same sp, ch 1, 3 dc in next sp, (ch 1, 3 dc in next sp, ch 2, 3 dc in same sp, ch 1, 3 dc in next sp) 3 times; join with sl st to top of ch-3; end.

SQUARE C (make 36)
With CC, work as for Square B.

BLOCK 1 (make 10)

Assembly
Refer to Block 1 Assembly Diagram. Use Square A. Shading indicates areas crocheted with MC.
With right sides facing, corresponding color, and sl st, catching outer lps only, crochet squares together. Work edging to complete block.

Edging
With right side facing, join CC in any corner sp.
Rnd 1: Ch 3 (first dc), 2 dc in sp, ch 2, 3 dc in same

sp, (ch 1, 3 dc), repeat between () into each sp and joining to corner, *ch 1, 3 dc in corner sp, ch 2, 3 dc in same sp, repeat between () into each sp and joining to corner, repeat from * 2 times more; join with sl st to top of ch-3.

Rnds 2–3: Sl st to corner sp, 2 sl st in sp, ch 3 (first dc), **turn**, 2 dc in sp, ch 2, 3 dc in same sp, (ch 1, 3 dc in next sp), repeat between () to corner, *ch 1, 3 dc in corner sp, ch 2, 3 dc in same sp, repeat between () to corner, repeat from * 2 times more; join with sl st to top of ch-3; end.

BLOCK 2 (make 8)
Work as for Block 1 **but** use **Block 2 Assembly Diagram** and work edging with MC.

BLOCK 3 (make 8)
Use Square B. Crochet squares together, in same manner as for Block 1, to form two 2-square rows. With CC, work edging as for Block 1.

BLOCK 4 (make 9)
Work as for Block 3 **but** use Square C and work edging with MC.

AFGHAN ASSEMBLY
Refer to Afghan Assembly Diagram. Crochet blocks together in same manner as for squares.

AFGHAN BORDER
With right side facing, join MC in any corner sp.
Rnds 1–2: Work Rnds 1–2 of Block Edging around entire outer edge of afghan.
Rnds 3–6: Repeat Rnd 2; **don't** end.
Rnd 7: Ch 1, **turn,** sc in each st and sp around, making 3 sc in each corner sp; join with sl st to first sc.
Rnd 8: Ch 1, **don't** turn, work a reverse sl st in each st of previous rnd; join with sl st to first reverse sl st; end. Secure and trim loose ends.

WINDMILLS BLOCK ASSEMBLY DIAGRAMS

Block 1

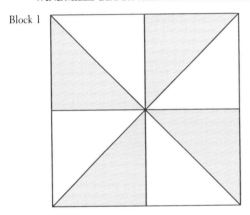

Block 2

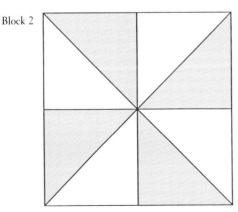

Shading indicates areas crocheted with MC.

WINDMILLS AFGHAN ASSEMBLY DIAGRAM

1	3	2	3	1
4	1	3	1	4
2	4	1	4	2
3	2	4	2	3
2	4	1	4	2
4	1	3	1	4
1	3	2	3	1

Two Hearts

Beginner

*Make every day Valentine's Day for someone who
holds a special place in your heart!
Single crochet and cross-stitch embroidery
are used in this portable project.*

SIZE
60″ × 72″

MATERIALS
Phildar Leader (worsted-weight acrylic), 3½ oz/216 yd
   balls: 11 balls White (A); 7 balls Fuchsia (B); 2 balls
   Purple (C)
Size K/10½ crochet hook (or size for gauge)
Yarn needle

GAUGE
Each square = 11⅞″

SEE
Cross-stitch Embroidery, Reverse Slip Stitch, Surface
Slip Stitch, and Working into One Loop Only

THE AFGHAN

BASIC SQUARE (make 30)
With A, ch 33.
Row 1: Sc in 2nd ch from hook and each ch across—
32 sts.
Rows 2–41: Ch 1, turn, sc in first st and each st across;
end.

EMBROIDERY
The design is worked in cross-stitch embroidery. Use
the yarn needle and a single strand of yarn. **Refer to
Embroidery Chart.**

TWO HEARTS EMBROIDERY CHART

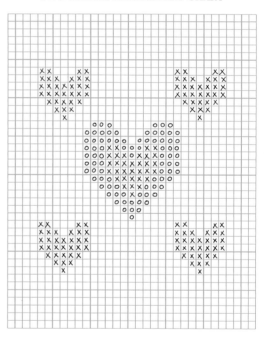

Each block = 1 stitch and row
(count turning ch as 1 st when embroidering)
× = B
o = C

SQUARE 1 (make 6)
Embroider entire chart.

SQUARE 2 (make 4)
Embroider only a large, two-color heart at the center.

SQUARE 3 (make 10)
Embroider only a small, B-colored heart at the center.

SQUARE 4 (make 10)
Leave remaining squares plain.

SQUARE BORDER
With right side facing, join A.

Rnd 1: Work a rnd of sc around entire square, having 32 sc evenly spaced along each side and making 3 sc at each corner; join with sl st to first sc; end.

Rnd 2: With right side facing, join C; sc in each st around, making 3 sc at each corner; join with sl st to first sc; end.

Rnd 3: With right side facing, join B; working into back lp only, sc in each st around, making 3 sc at each corner; join with sl st to first sc.

Rnds 4–7: Ch 1, **don't** turn, continuing with B and working into both lps, sc in each st around, making 3 sc at each corner; join with sl st to first sc; end.

ASSEMBLY
Refer to Assembly Diagram. With right sides facing, B, and overcast st, sew squares together following diagram.

EDGING
With right side facing, join B.

Rnd 1: Work a rnd of sc evenly around entire piece, making 3 sc at each corner; join with sl st to first sc.

Rnd 2: Ch 1, **don't** turn, work a reverse sl st in each st of previous rnd; join with sl st to first reverse sl st.

Rnd 3: Ch 1, **don't** turn, working below previous rnd, work a rnd of surface sl st around posts of sts of Rnd 1; join with sl st to first surface sl st; end.

Secure and trim loose ends.

TWO HEARTS ASSEMBLY DIAGRAM

1	3	4	3	1
3	4	1	4	3
4	2	3	2	4
4	2	3	2	4
3	4	1	4	3
1	3	4	3	1

Pine Tree

Intermediate

*Ever green and beautiful, a lone pine whispers
of woodlands and country lanes.
Basic and diagonal color-change granny squares
are used in this portable project.*

SIZE
55" × 55"

MATERIALS
Unger Utopia (worsted-weight acrylic), 3½ oz/240 yd
balls: 7 balls Black (A); 2 balls each Green (B) and
Teal (C); 1 ball Brown (D)
Size H/8 crochet hook (or size for gauge)

GAUGE
Each square = 2⅝"

SEE
Changing Color, Reverse Slip Stitch, and Working in
Rounds

NOTE
Joining slip stitch counts as last chain of round.

THE AFGHAN

SOLID-COLOR SQUARE
Ch 4; join with sl st to form ring.
Rnd 1 (right side): Ch 3 (first dc), 2 dc in ring, (ch
2, 3 dc in ring) 3 times, ch 1; join with sl st to top of
ch-3.
Rnd 2: Ch 3 (first dc), **turn,** 2 dc in sp, ch 2, 3 dc in
same sp, (ch 1, 3 dc in next sp, ch 2, 3 dc in same
sp) 3 times; join with sl st to top of ch-3; end.

TWO-COLOR SQUARE
With first color, ch 4; join with sl st to form ring.
Rnd 1 (right side): Ch 3 (first dc), 2 dc in ring, ch 2,
3 dc in ring, ch 1; with **second color (don't** end first
color), ch 1, 3 dc in ring, ch 2, 3 dc in ring, ch 1;
join with sl st to top of ch-3; **don't** end.
Rnd 2: Continuing with second color, ch 1, **turn,** sl
st in corner sp just completed, ch 3 (first dc), 2 dc in
sp, *ch 1, 3 dc in next sp, ch 2, 3 dc in same sp, ch
1, 3 dc in next sp, ch 1*; with **first color,** ch 1 (end
second color), 3 dc in same sp, repeat between *s; join
with sl st to top of ch-3; end.

SQUARE 1
Make **42** solid-color squares with A.

SQUARE 2
Make 8 solid-color squares with D.

SQUARE 3
Make 46 two-color squares using B for first color and
A for second color.

SQUARE 4
Make 44 two-color squares using C for first color and
A for second color.

SQUARE 5
Make **2** two-color squares using D for first color and
A for second color.

SQUARE 6
Make **2** two-color squares using B for first color and
D for second color.

ASSEMBLY

Refer to Assembly Diagram. With right sides facing, corresponding color, and sl st, catching outer lps only, crochet squares together to form vertical strips. Join vertical strips in same manner.

BORDER

With right side facing, join A in any corner sp.

Rnd 1: Ch 3 (first dc), 2 dc in sp, ch 2, 3 dc in same sp, (ch 1, 3 dc), repeat between () into each sp and joining to corner, *ch 1, 3 dc in corner sp, ch 2, 3 dc in same sp, repeat between () into each sp and joining to corner, repeat from * 2 times more; join with sl st to top of ch-3.

Rnds 2–8: Sl st to corner sp, 2 sl st in sp, ch 3 (first dc), **turn,** 2 dc in sp, ch 2, 3 dc in same sp, (ch 1, 3 dc in next sp), repeat between () to corner, *ch 1, 3 dc in corner sp, ch 2, 3 dc in same sp, repeat between () to corner, repeat from * 2 times more; join with sl st to top of ch-3; end after Rnd 8.

Rnd 9: With wrong side facing, join B in any corner sp; work as for Rnd 2, beginning with ch-3.

Rnd 10: Continuing with B, repeat Rnd 2; end.

Rnds 11–12: With C, repeat Rnds 9–10.

Rnds 13–14: With B, repeat Rnds 9–10.

Rnd 15: With A, repeat Rnd 9.

Rnds 16–22: Continuing with A, repeat Rnd 2; **don't** end.

Rnd 23: Ch 1, **turn,** sc in each st and sp around, making 3 sc in each corner sp; join with sl st to first sc.

Rnd 24: Ch 1, **don't** turn, work a reverse sl st in each st of previous rnd; join with sl st to first reverse sl st; end.

Secure and trim loose ends.

PINE TREE ASSEMBLY DIAGRAM

Two-color square orientation is indicated by diagonal line and color codes in corners.

Sunflowers

Beginner

*Bring the sunshine from a summer garden indoors!
Single crochet and cross-stitch embroidery are used
in this portable project.*

SIZE
47½″ × 57″

MATERIALS
Patons Canadiana (worsted-weight acrylic), 3½ oz/247
  yd balls: 5 balls each Off-white (A) and Brown (B);
  1 ball Rust (C); 2 balls Gold (D)
Size J/10 crochet hook (or size for gauge)
Yarn needle

GAUGE
Each square = 9⅜″

SEE
Cross-stitch Embroidery, Reverse Slip Stitch, Surface
Slip Stitch, and Working into One Loop Only

THE AFGHAN

BASIC SQUARE (make 30)
With A, ch 21.
Row 1: Sc in 2nd ch from hook and each ch across—
20 sts.
Rows 2–23: Ch 1, turn, sc in first st and each st across;
end.

EMBROIDERY
The design is worked in cross-stitch embroidery. Use
the yarn needle and a single strand of yarn. **Refer to
Embroidery Chart.** Embroider every square following
chart.

SUNFLOWERS EMBROIDERY CHART

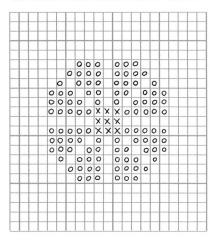

Each block = 1 stitch and row
(count turning ch as 1 st when embroidering)
× = B
o = D

SQUARE BORDER

With right side facing, join A.

Rnd 1: Work a rnd of sc around entire square, having 20 sc evenly spaced along each side and making 3 sc at each corner; join with sl st to first sc; end.

Rnd 2: With right side facing, join B; sc in each st around, making 3 sc at each corner; join with sl st to first sc.

Rnd 3: Ch 1, **don't** turn, continuing with B and working into back lp only, sc in each st around, making 3 sc at each corner; join with sl st to first sc; end.

Rnd 4: With right side facing, join C; work as for Rnd 3.

Rnd 5: With right side facing, join D; work as for Rnd 3.

Rnd 6: With right side facing, join B; work as for Rnd 3; **don't** end.

Rnds 7–8: Repeat Rnd 3; end.

ASSEMBLY

With right sides facing, B, and overcast st, sew squares together to form six 5-block rows.

EDGING

With right side facing, join B.

Rnd 1: Work a rnd of sc evenly around entire piece, making 3 sc at each corner; join with sl st to first sc.

Rnd 2: Ch 1, **don't** turn, work a reverse sl st in each st of previous rnd; join with sl st to first reverse sl st.

Rnd 3: Ch 1, **don't** turn, working below previous rnd, work a rnd of surface sl st around posts of sts of Rnd 1; join with sl st to first surface sl st; end.

Secure and trim loose ends.

Colonial
Charm

Ticking Stripe
Beginner

Narrow stripes have a classic look that's been popular since Colonial days. Double crochet is used in this quick-to-complete project.

SIZE
48½″ × 64½″ (before fringe)

MATERIALS
Unger Utopia (worsted-weight acrylic) 3½ oz/240 yd balls: 7 balls White (A); 6 balls Blue (B)
Size H/8 crochet hook (or size for gauge)

GAUGE
14 sts = 4″; 12 rows = 5″ (in pattern stitch)

SEE
Changing Color/End of Row and Fringe

NOTE
Afghan is worked from side to side rather than from top to bottom.

ONE-PIECE AFGHAN

With A, ch 227.
Row 1: Dc in 4th ch from hook and each ch across—225 sts.
Row 2: With B, ch 3 (first dc), turn, sk first st, dc in each st across.
Row 3: With A, repeat Row 2.
Repeat Rows 2–3, ending with Row 3, until piece measures 48″ from beginning; end.

EDGING
With right side facing and A, work a rnd of sc evenly around entire piece, making 3 sc at each corner; join with sl st to first sc; end.
Secure and trim loose ends.

FRINGE
Cut 12″ lengths of A. With wrong side facing, using 3 strands together for each fringe, attach fringe at each A-colored stripe across short edge of afghan. Repeat on other side.

Wedding Ring

Experienced

Bright with the promise of eternal love, this adaptation of a quilt favorite would make a treasured wedding gift. Basic and diagonal color-change granny squares are used in this portable project.

SIZE
57" × 57"

MATERIALS
Phildar Leader (worsted-weight acrylic), 3½ oz/216 yd balls: 6 balls White (A); 7 balls Navy (B); 1 ball each Pink (C), Red (D), Green (E), Turquoise (F), and Royal Blue (G)

Size H/8 crochet hook (or size for gauge)

GAUGE
Each square = 2"

SEE
Changing Color, Reverse Slip Stitch, and Working in Rounds

NOTE
Joining slip stitch counts as last chain of round.

THE AFGHAN

SOLID-COLOR SQUARE
Ch 4; join with sl st to form ring.

Rnd 1 (right side): Ch 3 (first dc), 2 dc in ring, (ch 1, 3 dc in ring) 3 times, ch 1; join with sl st to top of ch-3.

Rnd 2: Ch 3 (first dc), **turn**, 2 dc in sp, ch 2, 3 dc in same sp, (ch 1, 3 dc in next sp, ch 2, 3 dc in same sp) 3 times; join with sl st to top of ch-3; end.

TWO-COLOR SQUARE
With first color, ch 4; join with sl st to form ring.

Rnd 1 (right side): Ch 3 (first dc), 2 dc in ring, ch 2, 3 dc in ring, ch 1; with **second color** (**don't** end first color), ch 1, 3 dc in ring, ch 2, 3 dc in ring, ch 1; join with sl st to top of ch-3; **don't** end.

Rnd 2: Continuing with second color, ch 1, **turn**, sl st in corner sp just completed, ch 3 (first dc), 2 dc in sp, *ch 1, 3 dc in next sp, ch 2, 3 dc in same sp, ch 1, 3 dc in next sp, ch 1*; with **first color,** ch 1 (end second color), 3 dc in same sp, repeat between *s; join with sl st to top of ch-3; end.

SQUARE 1
Make 140 solid-color squares with A.

SQUARE 2
Make 8 two-color squares using C for first color and A for second color.

SQUARE 3
Make 8 two-color squares using D for first color and A for second color.

SQUARE 4
Make 8 two-color squares using F for first color and A for second color.

SQUARE 5
Make 8 two-color squares using G for first color and A for second color.

SQUARE 6
Make 10 two-color squares using D for first color and B for second color.

WEDDING RING ASSEMBLY DIAGRAM

Two-color square orientation is indicated by diagonal line and color codes in corners.

SQUARE 7
Make **10** two-color squares using E for first color and B for second color.

SQUARE 8
Make **5** two-color squares using F for first color and B for second color.

SQUARE 9
Make **15** two-color squares using B for first color and C for second color.

SQUARE 10
Make **2** two-color squares using D for first color and C for second color.

SQUARE 11
Make **5** two-color squares using F for first color and C for second color.

SQUARE 12
Make **15** two-color squares using E for first color and D for second color.

SQUARE 13
Make **5** two-color squares using G for first color and D for second color.

SQUARE 14
Make **10** two-color squares using C for first color and E for second color.

SQUARE 15
Make **5** two-color squares using G for first color and E for second color.

SQUARE 16
Make **2** two-color squares using F for first color and G for second color.

ASSEMBLY
Refer to Assembly Diagram. With right sides facing, corresponding color and sl st, catching outer lps only, crochet squares together to form vertical strips. Join vertical strips in same manner.

BORDER
With right side facing, join A in any corner sp.
Rnd 1: Ch 3 (first dc), 2 dc in sp, ch 2, 3 dc in same sp, (ch 1, 3 dc), repeat between () into each sp and joining to corner, *ch 1, 3 dc in corner sp, ch 2, 3 dc in same sp, repeat between () into each sp and joining to corner, repeat from * 2 times more; join with sl st to top of ch-3.
Rnds 2–8: Sl st to corner sp, 2 sl st in sp, ch 3 (first dc), **turn,** 2 dc in sp, ch 2, 3 dc in same sp, (ch 1, 3 dc in next sp), repeat between () to corner, *ch 1, 3 dc in corner sp, ch 2, 3 dc in same sp, repeat between () to corner, repeat from * 2 times more; join with sl st to top of ch-3; end after Rnd 8.
Rnd 9: With wrong side facing, join B in any corner sp; work as for Rnd 2, beginning with ch-3.
Rnds 10–24: Repeat Rnd 2; **don't** end.
Rnd 25: Ch 1, **turn,** sc in each st and sp around, making 3 sc in each corner sp; join with sl st to first sc.
Rnd 26: Ch 1, **don't** turn, work a reverse sl st in each st of previous rnd; join with sl st to first reverse sl st; end.
Secure and trim loose ends.

Colonial Star

Beginner

*Before city lights, long-ago nights were brightened
by a million stars. No wonder our Colonial ancestors
were fascinated by the symbol! Single crochet and cross-stitch
embroidery are used in this quick-to-complete project.*

SIZE
47" × 63" (before fringe)

MATERIALS
Lion Brand Jiffy (chunky-weight, brushed Orlon) 2½ oz/115 yd balls: 19 balls Blue Varigated (MC); 3 oz/ 135 yd balls: 1 ball Rose (A); 3 balls Cream (B)
Size K/10½ crochet hook (or size for gauge)
Yarn needle

GAUGE
24 sts = 7"; 23 rows = 5" (in pattern stitch)

SEE
Changing Color/End of Row, Cross-stitch Embroidery, and Fringe

ONE-PIECE AFGHAN
With MC, ch 161.
Row 1: Sc in 2nd ch from hook and each ch across—160 sts.
Rows 2–8: Ch 1, turn, sc in first st and each st across.
Row 9 (wrong side): With A, repeat Row 2.
Rows 10–32: With B, repeat Row 2.
Row 33: With A, repeat Row 2.
With MC only, repeat Row 2 until piece measures 55½" from beginning, ending with right-side row. Repeat Rows 9–33 one time more. With MC only repeat Row 2 eight times more; end.

EMBROIDERY
The design is worked in cross-stitch embroidery across the B-colored border panel. Use the yarn needle and a single strand of yarn. **Refer to Embroidery Chart.** Work the chart, repeating as indicated. Repeat on other side.

COLONIAL STAR EMBROIDERY CHART

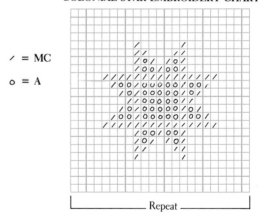

/ = MC

o = A

|—— Repeat ——|

Each block = 1 stitch and row
(count turning ch as 1 st when embroidering)

EDGING
With right side facing and MC, work a rnd of sc evenly around entire piece, making 3 sc at each corner; join with sl st to first sc; end. Secure and trim loose ends.

FRINGE
Cut 12" lengths of MC. With wrong side facing, using 3 strands together for each fringe, attach fringe at corner and at every 3rd st across short edge of afghan. Repeat on other side.

Homespun Texture

Beginner

*Texture's just right for coziness both day
and night. A single and double crochet seed pattern
is used in this quick-to-complete project.*

SIZE
46″ × 64″ (before fringe)

MATERIALS
Brunswick Boothbay (chunky-weight acrylic) 3 oz/120
  yd balls: 15 balls Tan (MC); 6 balls Ecru (CC)
Size K/10½ crochet hook (or size for gauge)

GAUGE
16 sts = 5″; 18 rows = 5″ (in pattern stitch)

SEE
Changing Color/End of Row, Fringe, Seed Pattern,
and Working into One Loop Only

NOTE
Afghan is worked from side to side rather than from
top to bottom.

ONE-PIECE AFGHAN

With MC, ch 204.
Base Row: Sc in 2nd ch from hook and each ch
across—203 sts.
Row 1 (wrong side): Ch 1, turn, sc in front lp only
of first st and each st across.
Row 2: Ch 1, turn, sc in both lps of first st, *sk next
st current row, dc in unused lp of sc 1 row below, sc
in both lps of next st current row, repeat from * across.
Row 3: Repeat Row 1.

Row 4: Ch 1, turn, sk first st current row, dc in unused
lp of sc 1 row below, *sc in both lps of next st current
row, sk next st current row, dc in unused lp of sc 1
row below, repeat from * across.
Rows 5–24: Repeat Rows 1–4.
Row 25: With CC, repeat Row 1.
Row 26: With CC, ch 1, turn, sc in both lps of first
st and each st across.
Row 27: With CC, repeat Row 1.
Row 28: With MC, repeat Row 2.
Rows 29–32: Repeat Rows 25–28.
Rows 33–34: Repeat Rows 25–26.
Repeat Rows 1–28 one time more, Rows 25–28 eight
times, then Rows 25–34 one time. Repeat Rows 1–34
one time, then Rows 1–24 one time. With MC, repeat
Row 26; end.

EDGING
With right side facing and MC, work a rnd of sc evenly
around entire piece, making 3 sc at each corner; join
with sl st to first sc; end.
Secure and trim loose ends.

FRINGE
Cut 12″ lengths of MC. With wrong side facing, using
3 strands together for each fringe, attach fringe at corner and at every 4th st across short edge of afghan.
Repeat on other side.

Flower Basket

Intermediate

*A tisket, a tasket . . . perky posies peek from
stylized baskets. Basic and diagonal color-change
granny squares are used in this portable project.*

SIZE
45" × 59"

MATERIALS
Patons Astra (sport-weight acrylic), 1¾ oz/182 yd balls:
   13 balls Green (MC); 2 balls each Tan (A) and Pink
   (B); 1 ball Peach (C); 2 balls White (D)
Size F/5 crochet hook (or size for gauge)

GAUGE
Each square = 1¾"

SEE
Changing Color, Reverse Slip Stitch, and Working in
Rounds

NOTE
Joining slip stitch counts as last chain of round.

THE AFGHAN

SQUARE 1 (make 84)
With MC, ch 4; join with sl st to form ring.
Rnd 1 (right side): Ch 3 (first dc), 2 dc in ring, (ch
2, 3 dc in ring) 3 times, ch 1; join with sl st to top of
ch-3.
Rnd 2: Ch 3 (first dc), **turn**, 2 dc in sp, ch 2, 3 dc in
same sp, (ch 1, 3 dc in next sp, ch 2, 3 dc in same
sp) 3 times; join with sl st to top of ch-3; end.

SQUARE 2 (make 36)
With A, work as for Square 1.

SQUARE 3 (make 72)
With MC, ch 4; join with sl st to form ring.
Rnd 1 (right side): Ch 3 (first dc), 2 dc in ring, ch 2,
3 dc in ring, ch 1; with **B** (**don't** end MC), ch 1, 3
dc in ring, ch 2, 3 dc in ring, ch 1; join with sl st to
top of ch-3; end B.
Rnd 2: Join D in corner sp just completed; ch 3 (first
dc), **turn**, 2 dc in sp, *ch 1, 3 dc next sp, ch 2, 3 dc
in same sp, ch 1, 3 dc in next sp, ch 1*; with **MC**,
ch 1 (end D), 3 dc in same sp, repeat between *s; join
with sl st to top of ch-3; end.

SQUARE 4 (make 48)
Work as for Square 3 **but** use C where B is called for.

SQUARE 5 (make 60)
Work Rnd 1 as for Square 3 **but** use A where B is
called for; **don't** end A. Work Rnd 2 as for Square 3
but continue with A where D is called for, beginning
with ch-3.

BLOCK ASSEMBLY
Refer to Assembly Diagram. Shading indicates areas
crocheted with MC. With right sides facing, corresponding color, and sl st, catching outer lps only,
crochet squares together to form blocks.

BLOCK BORDER
With right side facing, join MC in any corner sp.
Rnd 1: Ch 3 (first dc), 2 dc in sp, ch 2, 3 dc in same
sp, (ch 1, 3 dc), repeat between () into each sp and

joining to corner, *ch 1, 3 dc in corner sp, ch 2, 3 dc in same sp, repeat between () into each sp and joining to corner, repeat from * 2 times more; join with sl st to top of ch-3.

Rnds 2–3: Sl st to corner sp, 2 sl st in sp, ch 3 (first dc), **turn,** 2 dc in sp, ch 2, 3 dc in same sp, (ch 1, 3 dc in next sp), repeat between () to corner, *ch 1, 3 dc in corner sp, ch 2, 3 dc in same sp, repeat between () to corner, repeat from * 2 times more; join with sl st to top of ch-3; end after Rnd 3.

Rnd 4: With right side facing, join B in any corner sp; work as for Rnd 2, beginning with ch-3; end.

Rnd 5: With wrong side facing and MC, work as for Rnd 4; **don't** end.

Rnd 6: Continuing with MC, repeat Rnd 2; end.

AFGHAN ASSEMBLY

Crochet blocks together, in same manner as for squares, to form four 3-block rows.

AFGHAN EDGING

With right side facing, join MC in any corner sp.

Rnds 1–2: Work Rnds 1 and 2 of Block Border around entire outer edge of afghan; **don't** end.

Rnd 3: Ch 1, **turn,** sc in each st and sp around, making 3 sc in each corner sp; join with sl st to first sc.

Rnd 4: Ch 1, **don't** turn, work a reverse sl st in each st of previous rnd; join with sl st to first reverse sl st; end.

Secure and trim loose ends.

FLOWER BASKET ASSEMBLY DIAGRAM

Shading indicates areas crocheted wih MC.

Calico

Beginner

Pattern play spells patchwork prettiness.
A single crochet mesh pattern
is used in this portable project.

SIZE
46″ × 61″

MATERIALS
Bernat Berella "4" (worsted-weight acrylic) 3½ oz/240
   yd balls: 4 balls Dark Rose (A); 3 balls each Green
   (B) and Pink (C); 4 balls Natural (D)
Size J/10 crochet hook (or size for gauge)

GAUGE
Each square = 7½″

SEE
Changing Color/End of Row, Reverse Slip Stitch, Surface Slip Stitch, and Working with Chain Spaces/In

THE AFGHAN

BASIC SQUARE PATTERN
Ch 32.
Row 1: Sc in 2nd ch from hook, *ch 1, sk next ch, sc in next ch, repeat from * across—31 sts (count includes each sc **and** ch-1 sp).
Row 2: Ch 1, turn, sc in first st, sc in first ch-1 sp, *ch 1, sk next st, sc in next ch-1 sp, repeat from * across, sc in last st.
Row 3: Ch 1, turn, sc in first st, *ch 1, sk next st, sc in next ch-1 sp, repeat from * across, end with sc in last st (rather than ch-1 sp).
Rows 4–31: Repeat Rows 2–3; end.

Using the basic square pattern, make 2 each of every square, following stripe patterns below.

STRIPE PATTERN I
1 row first color, *1 row second color, 1 row first color, repeat from *.

Square 1
Use A for first color, D for second color.

Square 2
Use B for first color, D for second color.

Square 3
Use B for first color, C for second color.

Square 4
Use C for first color, A for second color.

STRIPE PATTERN II
1 row first color, *1 row second color, 2 rows first color, repeat from *.

Square 5
Use A for first color, D for second color.

Square 6
Use D for first color, A for second color.

Square 7
Use B for first color, D for second color.

Square 8
Use D for first color, B for second color.

STRIPE PATTERN III

1 row first color, *2 rows second color, 2 rows third color, 2 rows first color, repeat from *.

Square 9

Use A for first color, D for second color, and C for third color.

Square 10

Use B for first color, C for second color, and D for third color.

Square 11

Use C for first color, B for second color, and A for third color.

Square 12

Use D for first color, A for second color, and B for third color.

STRIPE PATTERN IV

2 rows first color, *1 row second color, 1 row third color, 1 row second color, 3 rows first color, repeat from *, end with 2 rows first color (rather than 3).

Square 13

Use A for first color, C for second color, and B for third color.

Square 14

Use A for first color, D for second color, and B for third color.

Square 15

Use B for first color, D for second color, and A for third color.

Square 16

Use C for first color, A for second color, and B for third color.

Square 17

Use D for first color, A for second color, and C for third color.

Square 18

Use D for first color, B for second color, and C for third color.

STRIPE PATTERN V

2 rows first color, *1 row second color, 1 row first color, 1 row third color, 3 rows first color, repeat from *, end with 2 rows first color (rather than 3).

Square 19

Use A for first color, B for second color, and D for third color.

Square 20

Use D for first color, B for second color, and A for third color.

Square 21

Use A for first color, B for second color, and C for third color.

Square 22

Use C for first color, B for second color, and A for third color.

Square 23

Use C for first color, B for second color, and D for third color.

Square 24

Use D for first color, B for second color, and C for third color.

ASSEMBLY

Refer to Assembly Diagram. With right sides facing, corresponding color, and overcast st, sew squares together following diagram.

EDGING

With right side facing, join B.

Rnd 1: Work a rnd of sc evenly around entire piece, making 3 sc at each corner; join with sl st to first sc.

Rnd 2: Ch 1, **don't** turn, work a reverse sl st in each st of previous rnd; join with sl st to first reverse sl st.

Rnd 3: Ch 1, **don't** turn, working below previous rnd, work a rnd of surface sl st around posts of sts of Rnd 1; join with sl st to first surface sl st; end.

Secure and trim loose ends.

CALICO ASSEMBLY DIAGRAM

2	11	24	13	10	6
21	18	9	1	16	19
12	5	15	22	8	3
23	17	4	7	14	20
6	10	13	24	11	2
19	16	1	9	18	21
3	8	22	15	5	12
20	14	7	4	17	23

Rosebuds

Beginner

Gather the diminutive blossoms of a floral coverlet!
Single crochet and cross-stitch embroidery
are used in this portable project.

SIZE
44½″ × 62″

MATERIALS
Unger Utopia (worsted-weight acrylic), 3½ oz/240 yd
   balls: 12 balls White (MC); 1 ball each Rose (A),
   Pink (B), and Green (C)
Size J/10 crochet hook (or size for gauge)
Yarn needle

GAUGE
Each square = 8¾″

SEE
Cross-stitch Embroidery, Reverse Slip Stitch, and Surface Slip Stitch

THE AFGHAN

BASIC SQUARE (make 35)
With MC, ch 33.
Row 1: Sc in 2nd ch from hook and each ch across—
32 sts.
Rows 2–36: Ch 1, turn, sc in first st and each st across;
end.

EMBROIDERY
The design is worked in cross-stitch embroidery. Use
the yarn needle and a single strand of yarn.

SQUARE 1 (make 13)
Refer to Embroidery Chart 1. Embroider following
chart.

SQUARE 2 (make 14)
Refer to Embroidery Chart 2. Embroider following
chart.

SQUARE 3 (make 8)
Leave remaining squares plain.

ASSEMBLY
Refer to Assembly Diagram. With right sides facing,
MC, and overcast st, sew squares together following
diagram.

EDGING
With right side facing, join MC.
Rnd 1: Work a rnd of sc evenly around entire piece,
making 3 sc at each corner; join with sl st to first sc.
Rnd 2: Ch 1, **don't** turn, work a reverse sl st in each
st of previous rnd; join with sl st to first reverse sl st.
Rnd 3: Ch 1, **don't** turn, working below previous rnd,
work a rnd of surface sl st around posts of sts of Rnd
1; join with sl st to first surface sl st; end.
Secure and trim loose ends.

ROSEBUDS EMBROIDERY CHARTS

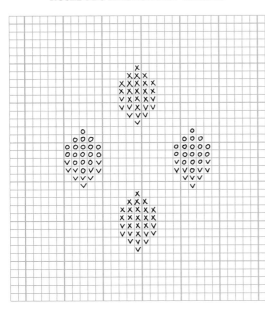

CHART 1

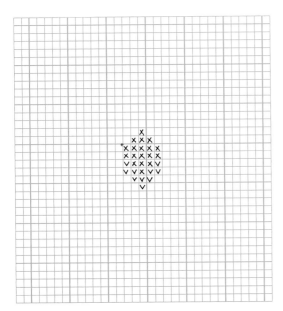

CHART 2

Each block = 1 stitch and row
(count turning ch as 1 st when embroidering)
× = A
o = B
v = C

ROSEBUDS ASSEMBLY DIAGRAM

1	3	2	3	1
3	2	1	2	3
2	1	2	1	2
1	2	1	2	1
2	1	2	1	2
3	2	1	2	3
1	3	2	3	1

Kites

Beginner

*Colorful kites soar on a background as gray as
a windy March sky. Basic and diagonal color-change
granny squares are used in this portable project.*

SIZE
57″ × 77″

MATERIALS
Coats & Clark Red Heart Super Saver (worsted-weight
acrylic), 8 oz/480 yd skeins: 6 skeins Light Blue
(MC); 1 skein each White (A), Navy (B), Green (C),
and Red (D)
Size H/8 crochet hook (or size for gauge)

GAUGE
Each square = 5″

SEE
Changing Color, Reverse Slip Stitch, and Working in
Rounds

NOTE
Joining slip stitch counts as last chain of round.

THE AFGHAN

SOLID-COLOR SQUARE (make 68)
With MC, ch 4; join with sl st to form ring.
Rnd 1 (right side): Ch 3 (first dc), 2 dc in ring, (ch
2, 3 dc in ring) 3 times, ch 1; join with sl st to top of
ch-3.
Rnd 2: Ch 3 (first dc), **turn,** 2 dc in sp, ch 2, 3 dc in
same sp, (ch 1, 3 dc in next sp, ch 2, 3 dc in same
sp) 3 times; join with sl st to top of ch-3.
Rnd 3: Sl st to corner sp, 2 sl st in sp, ch 3 (first dc),
turn, 2 dc in sp, ch 2, 3 dc in same sp, ch 1, 3 dc in
next sp, (ch 1, 3 dc in next sp, ch 2, 3 dc in same sp,
ch 1, 3 dc in next sp) 3 times; join with sl st to top of
ch-3.
Rnd 4: Work as for Rnd 3, making 1 more 3-dc group
per side; end.

MULTICOLOR SQUARE (make 72)
With MC, ch 4; join with sl st to form ring.
Rnd 1 (right side): Ch 3 (first dc), 2 dc in ring, ch 2,
3 dc in ring, ch 1; with **A** (**don't** end MC), ch 1, 3
dc in ring, ch 2, 3 dc in ring, ch 1; join with sl st to
top of ch-3; end A.
Rnd 2: Join B in corner sp just completed; ch 3 (first
dc), **turn,** 2 dc in sp, *ch 1, 3 dc in next sp, ch 2, 3
dc in same sp, ch 1, 3 dc in next sp, ch 1*; with **MC**,
ch 1 (end B), 3 dc in same sp, repeat between *s; join
with sl st to top of ch-3; **don't** end.
Rnd 3: Continuing with MC, ch 1, **turn,** sl st in corner
sp just completed, ch 3 (first dc), 2 dc in sp, *(ch 1,
3 dc in next sp) 2 times, ch 2, 3 dc in same sp, repeat
between () 2 times more, ch 1*; with **C** (**don't** end
MC), ch 1, 3 dc in same sp, repeat between *s; join
with sl st to top of ch 3; end C.
Rnd 4: Join D in corner sp just completed; ch 3 (first
dc), **turn,** 2 dc in sp, *(ch 1, 3 dc in next sp) 3 times,
ch 2, 3 dc in same sp, repeat between () 3 times more,
ch 1*; with **MC**, ch 1, (end D), 3 dc in same sp,
repeat between *s; join with sl to top of ch-3; end.

KITES ASSEMBLY DIAGRAM

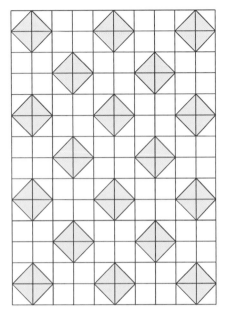

Shading indicates multicolored areas.

ASSEMBLY

Refer to Assembly Diagram. Shading indicates multicolored areas. With right sides facing, corresponding color, and sl st, catching outer lps only, crochet squares together to form vertical strips. Join vertical strips in same manner.

BORDER

With right side facing, join MC in any corner sp.

Rnd 1: Ch 3 (first dc), 2 dc in sp, ch 2, 3 dc in same sp, (ch 1, 3 dc), repeat between () into each sp and joining to corner, *ch 1, 3 dc in corner sp, ch 2, 3 dc in same sp, repeat between () into each sp and joining to corner, repeat from * 2 times more; join with sl st to top of ch-3.

Rnd 2: Sl st to corner sp, 2 sl st in sp, ch 3 (first dc), **turn,** 2 dc in sp, ch 2, 3 dc in same sp, (ch 1, 3 dc in next sp), repeat between () to corner, *ch 1, 3 dc in corner sp, ch 2, 3 dc in same sp, repeat between () to corner, repeat from * 2 times more; join with sl st to top of ch-3; end.

Rnd 3: With wrong side facing, join B in any corner sp; work as for Rnd 2, beginning with ch-3; end.

Rnd 4: With right side facing and C, work as for Rnd 3.

Rnd 5: With D, repeat Rnd 3.

Rnd 6: With MC, repeat Rnd 4; **don't** end.

Rnd 7: Continuing with MC, repeat Rnd 2; **don't** end.

Rnd 8: Ch 1, **don't** turn, sc in each st and sp around, making 3 sc in each corner sp; join with sl st to first sc.

Rnd 9: Ch 1, **don't** turn, work a reverse sl st in each st of previous rnd; join with sl st to first reverse sl st; end.

Secure and trim loose ends.

Timeless Traditional

Lotus

Beginner

The elegance of the lotus will add a hint of Eastern mystery to your decor. Single crochet and cross-stitch embroidery are used in this project.

SIZE

49" × 60" (before fringe)

MATERIALS

Reynolds Reynelle Deluxe (worsted-weight Orlon) 3½ oz/240 yd balls: 12 balls Purple (MC); 1 ball each White (A), Pink (B), and Gray (C)
Size J/10 crochet hook (or size for gauge)
Yarn needle

GAUGE

17 sts = 5"; 23 rows = 6" (in pattern stitch)

SEE

Cross stitch Embroidery and Fringe

ONE-PIECE AFGHAN

With MC, ch 167.
Row 1: Sc in 2nd ch from hook and each ch across—166 sts.
Row 2: Ch 1, turn, sc in first st and each st across. With MC only, repeat Row 2 until piece measures 59½" from beginning; end.

EMBROIDERY

The design is worked in cross-stitch embroidery across the short edge of the afghan. Use the yarn needle and a single strand of yarn. **Refer to Embroidery Chart.** Leaving the edge stitch of both sides and the first 5 rows unembroidered, work the chart, beginning and repeating as indicated. Repeat on other side.

EDGING

With right side facing and MC, work a rnd of sc evenly around entire piece, making 3 sc at each corner; join with sl st to first sc; end. Secure and trim loose ends.

FRINGE

Cut 12" lengths of MC. With wrong side facing, using 3 strands together for each fringe, attach fringe at corner and at every 3rd st across short edge of afghan. Repeat on other side.

LOTUS EMBROIDERY CHART

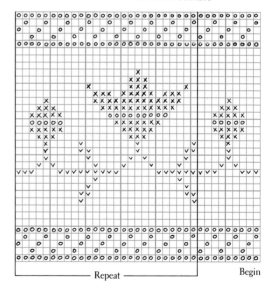

Each block = 1 stitch and row
(count turning ch as 1 st when embroidering)
x = A
o = B
v = C

Fair Isle-Style Sampler

Experienced

*Add a whisper of softness to a room with the
misty dawn colors of an exquisitely patterned coverlet.
Double crochet carried-thread color work
is used in this portable project.*

SIZE
46″ × 64″

MATERIALS
Brunswick Windmist (worsted-weight, brushed Orlon and acrylic blend) 1¾ oz/135 yd balls: 13 balls White (MC); 5 balls Blue (A); 3 balls each Green (B) and Rose (C)
Size H/8 crochet hook (or size for gauge)

GAUGE
Each square = 9″

SEE
Changing Color and Reverse Slip Stitch

THE AFGHAN

SQUARE 1 (make 5)
With MC, ch 36.
Row 1 (wrong side): Dc in 4th ch from hook and each ch across—34 sts.
Rows 2–4: Ch 3 (first dc), turn, sk first st, dc in each st across.
Refer to Stitch Chart 1.
Row 5: Work Chart Row 5 as follows: With MC, ch 3 (first dc), turn, sk first st, dc in next 15 sts; with A, dc in next 2 sts; with MC, dc in last 16 sts.
Work Chart Rows 6–17 in same manner; end.

SQUARE 2 (make 5)
Work as for Square 1 through Row 1.

Refer to Stitch Chart 2.
Row 2: Work Chart Row 2 as follows: With MC, ch 3 (first dc), turn, sk first st, dc in next 15 sts; with A, dc in next 2 sts; with MC, dc in last 16 sts.
Work Chart Rows 3–17 in same manner; end.

SQUARE 3 (make 5)
Work as for Square 1 through Row 1.
Refer to Stitch Chart 3.
Row 2: Work Chart Row 2 as follows: With A, ch 3 (first dc), turn, sk first st, dc in next st; (with MC, dc in next 14 sts; with A, dc in next 2 sts) 2 times.
Work Chart Rows 3–17 in same manner; end.

SQUARE 4 (make 5)
Work as for Square 1 through Row 1.
Refer to Stitch Chart 4.
Row 2: Work Chart Row 2 as follows: With MC, ch 3 (first dc), turn, sk first st, dc in next 3 sts; with A, dc in next 2 sts; (with MC, dc in next 10 sts; with A, dc in next 2 sts) 2 times; with MC, dc in last 4 sts.
Work Chart Rows 3–17 in same manner; end.

SQUARE 5 (make 5)
Work as for Square 1 through Row 1.
Row 2: With A, ch 3 (first dc), turn, sk first st, dc in next st; *with B, dc in next 2 sts; with A, dc in next 2 sts, repeat from * across.
Row 3: With MC, ch 3 (first dc), turn, sk first st, dc in each st across.

FAIR ISLE–STYLE SAMPLER STITCH CHARTS

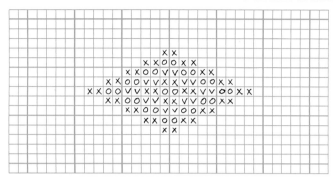

CHART 1

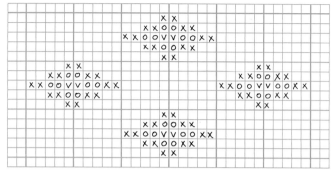

CHART 2

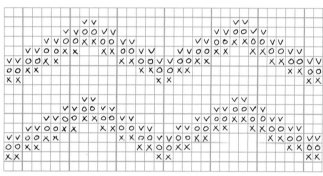

CHART 3

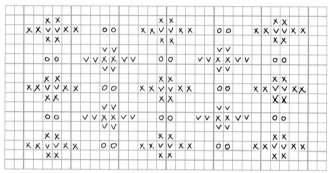

CHART 4

Each block = 1 stitch and row

☐ = MC
× = A
○ = B
∨ = C

Row 4: Work as for Row 2 **but** use C where B is called for.

Row 5: Repeat Row 3.

Row 6–17: Repeat Rows 2–5; end.

SQUARE 6 (make 5)

Work as for Square 1 through Row 1.

Row 2: With A, ch 3 (first dc), turn, sk first st, dc in next st; *with B, dc in next 2 sts; with A, dc in next 2 sts, repeat from * across.

Row 3: With C, ch 3 (first dc), turn, sk first st, dc in next st; *with A, dc in next 2 sts; with C, dc in next 2 sts, repeat from * across.

Row 4: Repeat Row 2.

Row 5: With MC, ch 3 (first dc), turn, sk first st, dc in each st across.

Rows 6–8: Work as for Rows 2–4 **but** use C where B is called for and B where C is called for.

Row 9: Repeat Row 5.

Rows 10–17: Repeat Rows 2–9; end.

SQUARE 7 (make 5)

Work as for Square 1 through Row 2.

Row 3: With MC, ch 3 (first dc), turn, dc in next 3 sts; with A, dc in next 2 sts; (with MC, dc in next 4 sts; with B, dc in next 2 sts; with MC, dc in next 4 sts; with A, dc in next 2 sts) 2 times; with MC, dc in last 4 sts.

Rows 4–5: With MC, ch 3 (first dc), turn, sk first st, dc in each st across.

Row 6: Work as for Row 3 **but** use C where A is called for and A where B is called for.

Row 7–8: Repeat Rows 4–5.

Rows 9–14: Repeat Rows 3–8.

Rows 15–17: Repeat Rows 3–5; end.

ASSEMBLY

Refer to Assembly Diagram. With right sides facing, MC, and overcast st, sew squares together following diagram.

EDGING

With right side facing, join A.

Rnd 1: Work a rnd of sc evenly around entire piece, making 3 sc at each corner; join with sl st to first sc.

Rnd 2: Ch 2 (first hdc), **don't** turn, sk first st, hdc in each st around, making 3 hdc at each corner; join with sl st to top of ch-2.

Rnd 3: Ch 1, **don't** turn, work a reverse sl st in each st of previous rnd; join with sl st to first reverse sl st; end.

Secure and trim loose ends.

FAIR ISLE–STYLE SAMPLER ASSEMBLY DIAGRAM

4	7	1	5	2
6	3	5	7	1
2	4	7	3	5
1	6	3	4	7
5	2	4	6	3
7	1	6	2	4
3	5	2	1	6

Latin Star

Experienced

Every night will be warm and starry with this richly textured afghan. Single crochet and triple crochet bobbles are used in this portable project.

SIZE
45″ × 62½″

MATERIALS
Patons Canadiana (worsted-weight acrylic), 1¾ oz/122 yd balls: 29 balls Peach
Size J/10 crochet hook (or size for gauge)

GAUGE
Each square = 8⅝″

SEE
Reverse Slip Stitch, Surface Slip Stitch, and Triple Crochet Bobbles

THE AFGHAN

SQUARE 1 (make 14)
Ch 34.
Row 1: Sc in 2nd ch from hook and each ch across—33 sts.
Row 2: Ch 1, turn, sc in first st and each st across.
Row 3 (wrong side): Ch 1, turn, sc in first st, sl st in next st, *tr in next st, sl st in next st, repeat from * across, sc in last st (**tr bobbles formed on right side of work**).
Row 4: Repeat Row 2.
Row 5: Ch 1, turn, sc in first st, *sl st in next st, tr in next st, sl st in next st*, sc in next 25 sts, repeat between *s 1 time more, sc in last st.
Row 6: Repeat Row 2.
Rows 7–34: Repeat Rows 5–6.

Row 35: Repeat Row 3.
Rows 36–38: Repeat Row 2; end.

SQUARE 2 (make 12)
Work Rows 1–6 as for Square 1.
Row 7: Ch 1, turn, sc in first st, *sl st in next st, tr in next st, sl st in next st, sc in next st, repeat from * across (**tr bobbles formed on right side of work**).
Rows 8–10: Repeat Rows 4–6.
Rows 11–34: Repeat Rows 7–10.
Work Rows 35–38 as for Square 1.

SQUARE 3 (make 9)
Work Rows 1–8 as for Square 1.
Refer to Stitch Chart.
Row 9: Work Chart Row 9 as follows: Ch 1, turn, sc in first st, *sl st in next st, tr in next st, sl st in next st*, (sc in next 11 sts, repeat between *s 1 time) 2 times, sc in last st.
Work Chart Rows 10–29 in same manner.
Work Rows 30–38 as for Square 1.

ASSEMBLY
Refer to Assembly Diagram. With right sides facing and overcast st, sew squares together following diagram.

EDGING
With right side facing, join yarn at upper right-hand corner.
Rnd 1: Work a rnd of sc evenly around entire piece, having an odd number of stitches along each edge and

making 3 sc at each corner; join with sl st to first sc.

Rnd 2: Ch 1, **don't** turn, sc in each st around, making 3 sc at each corner; join with sl st to first sc.

Rnd 3: Ch 1, **turn,** tr in joining, sl st in next st, tr in next st, *at corner, work sl st, tr, sl st in 2nd of 3 corner sc, tr in next st, (sl st in next st, tr in next st), repeat between () to corner, repeat from * 3 times more, sl st in last st; join with sl st to first tr.

Rnd 4: Ch 1, **turn,** and repeat Rnd 2.

Rnd 5: Repeat Rnd 2.

Rnd 6: Ch 1, **don't** turn, work a reverse sl st in each st of previous rnd; join with sl st to first reverse sl st.

Rnd 7: Ch 1, **don't** turn, working below previous rnd, work a rnd of surface sl st around posts of sts of Rnd 5; join with sl st to first surface sl st.

Rnd 8: Repeat Rnd 7; end.

Secure and trim loose ends.

LATIN STAR ASSEMBLY DIAGRAM

3	2	1	2	3
2	1	3	1	2
1	2	1	2	1
3	1	3	1	3
1	2	1	2	1
2	1	3	1	2
3	2	1	2	3

LATIN STAR STITCH CHART

Each block = 1 stitch and row

< * = Sl st

x * = Sc

‡ * = Tr

Row 29

Row 9 (wrong side)

*International Crochet Symbol

Dreamscape

Intermediate

*Apple blossoms and star-studded, rosy-hued evening skies
make for sweet dreams on an afghan as soft as a spring breeze.
Single crochet carried-thread color work and cross-stitch
embroidery are used in this quick-to-complete project.*

SIZE
47″ × 65″ (before fringe)

MATERIALS
Lion Brand Jiffy (chunky-weight, brushed Orlon) 2½
   oz/115 yd balls: 5 balls Blue Varigated (A); 3 oz/135
   yd balls: 16 balls Rose (B); 2 balls Cream (C); 1 ball
   Silver (D)
Size K/10½ crochet hook (or size for gauge)
Yarn needle

GAUGE
13 sts = 4″; 16 rows = 4″ (in pattern stitch)

SEE
Changing Color, Cross-stitch Embroidery, and Fringe

THE AFGHAN

ONE-PIECE AFGHAN
With A, ch 152.
Row 1: Sc in 2nd ch from hook and each ch across—
151 sts.
Rows 2–5: Ch 1, turn, sc in first st and each st across.
Rows 6–10: With B, repeat Row 2.
Rows 11–18: With A, repeat Row 2.
Row 19: With A, ch 1, turn, sc in first 11 sts; *with
B, sc in next 3 sts; with A, sc in next 11 sts, repeat
from * across.

Row 20: With B, ch 1, turn, sc in first st; with A, sc
in next 9 sts, *with B, sc in next 5 sts; with A, sc in
next 9 sts, repeat from * across; with B, sc in last st.
Row 21: With B, ch 1, turn, sc in first 2 sts; with A,
sc in next 7 sts; *with B, sc in next 7 sts; with A, sc
in next 7 sts, repeat from * across; with B, sc in last
2 sts.
Row 22: With B, ch 1, turn, sc in first 3 sts; with A,
sc in next 5 sts; *with B, sc in next 9 sts; with A, sc
in next 5 sts, repeat from * across; with B, sc in last
3 sts.
Row 23: With B, ch 1, turn, sc in first 4 sts; with A,
sc in next 3 sts; *with B sc in next 11 sts; with A, sc
in next 3 sts, repeat from * across; with B, sc in last
4 sts.
Rows 24–234: With B only, repeat Row 2.
Rows 235–256: Work Rows 2–23 in **reverse order** (begin with Row 23 and end with Row 2).
Row 257: Repeat Row 2; end.

EMBROIDERY
The design is worked in cross-stitch embroidery across
the short edge of the afghan. Use the yarn needle and
a single strand of yarn. **Refer to Embroidery Chart.**
Starting at Row 7, work the chart, beginning, repeating, and ending as indicated. Work Rows 8–75 in same
manner. Repeat Rows 36–75 one time, Rows 64–75

DREAMSCAPE EMBROIDERY CHART

Row 75

Row 66
Row 64

Row 36

Row 7

End — Repeat — Begin

two times, then Rows 64–66 one time. Turn afghan so opposite short edge is closest to you and work Rows 1–75. Repeat Rows 36–75 one time more.

EDGING
With right side facing and A, work a rnd of sc evenly around entire piece, making 3 sc at each corner; join with sl st to first sc; end.
Secure and trim loose ends.

FRINGE
Cut 12″ lengths of A. With wrong side facing, using 3 strands together for each fringe, attach fringe at corner and at every 3rd st across short edge of afghan. Repeat on other side.

Each block = 1 stitch and row
(don't count turning ch as st when embroidering)
O = A
X = C
V = D

Art Greco

Intermediate

Summery white and the blue of the Aegean,
in a classic key design,
suggest the romance of the Greek Isles.
Double crochet carried-thread
color work is used in this project.

SIZE
53½″ × 63½″

MATERIALS
Coats & Clark Red Heart Luster Sheen (sport-weight acrylic) 2 oz/180 yd skeins: 16 skeins Aqua (MC); 4 skeins White (CC)
Size F/5 crochet hook (or size for gauge)

GAUGE
23 sts = 5″; 11 rows = 5″ (in pattern stitch)

SEE
Changing Color and Reverse Slip Stitch

ONE-PIECE AFGHAN

With MC, ch 244.
Base Row: Dc in 4th ch from hook and each ch across—242 sts.
Next Row: Ch 3 (first dc), turn, sk first st, dc in each st across.
Repeat the last row 2 times more; end.
Refer to Stitch Chart.
Row 1: With CC, ch 3 (first dc), turn, sk first st, dc in each st across.

ART GRECO STITCH CHART

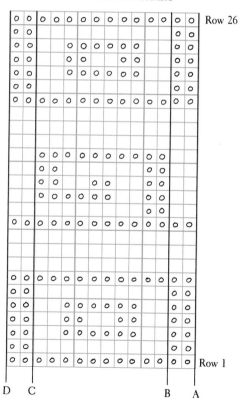

Each block = 1 stitch and row
□ = MC
o = CC

Row 2 (right side): Work Chart Row 2 as follows: From A *to* B: with CC, ch 3 (first dc), turn, sk first st, dc in next st; then from B *to* D: (with MC, dc in next 10 sts; with CC, dc in next 2 sts) 20 times.

Row 3: Work Chart Row 3 as follows: From D *to* C: with CC, ch 3 (first dc), turn, sk first st, dc in next st; then from C *to* A: (with MC, dc in next 2 sts; with CC, dc in next 6 sts; with MC, dc in next 2 sts; with CC, dc in next 2 sts) 20 times.

Work Chart Rows 4–26 in same manner.

With MC only, work in dc until piece measures 49″ from beginning, ending with wrong-side row.

Work Chart Rows 1–26 in **reverse** order (begin with Row 26 and end with Row 1).

With MC only, work in dc for 4 rows; end.

EDGING

With right side facing, join MC.

Rnd 1: Work a rnd of sc evenly around entire piece, making 3 sc at each corner; join with sl st to first sc.

Rnd 2: Ch 2 (first hdc), **don't** turn, sk first st, hdc in each st around, making 3 hdc at each corner; join with sl st to top of ch-2.

Rnd 3: Ch 1, **don't** turn, work a reverse sl st in each st of previous rnd; join with sl st to first reverse sl st; end.

Secure and trim loose ends.

Roman Stripe

Intermediate

Shifting stripes suggest sunlight and shadows.
Double crochet carried-thread color work
is used in this quick-to-complete project.

SIZE
50½″ × 67½″

MATERIALS
Bernat Berella "4" (worsted-weight acrylic) 3½ oz/240
  yd balls: 7 balls Brown (MC); 2 balls each Terracotta
  (A), Gray (B), White (C), and Tan (D)
Size H/8 crochet hook (or size for gauge)

GAUGE
17 sts = 5″; 9 rows = 5″ (in pattern stitch)

SEE
Changing Color/Within a Row and Reverse Slip Stitch

ONE-PIECE AFGHAN

With MC, ch 172.
Base Row: Dc in 4th ch from hook and each ch
across—170 sts.

Refer to Stitch Chart.
Row 1 (right side): Work Chart Row 1 from **right to
left** as follows: With MC, ch 3 (first dc), turn, sk first
st, dc in next st; *with A, dc in next 10 sts; with MC,
dc in next 2 sts; (with B, dc in next 2 sts; with MC,
dc in next 2 sts) 3 times, repeat from * across.
Row 2: Work Chart Row 2 from **left to right,** keeping
to pattern established in last right-side row.
Work Chart Rows 3–24 in same manner.
Repeat Rows 1–24 four times more; end.

EDGING
With right side facing, join MC.
Rnd 1: Work a rnd of sc evenly around entire piece,
making 3 sc at each corner; join with sl st to first sc.
Rnd 2: Ch 1, **don't** turn, work a reverse sl st in each
st of previous rnd; join with sl st to first reverse sl st;
end.
Secure and trim loose ends.

ROMAN STRIPE STITCH CHART

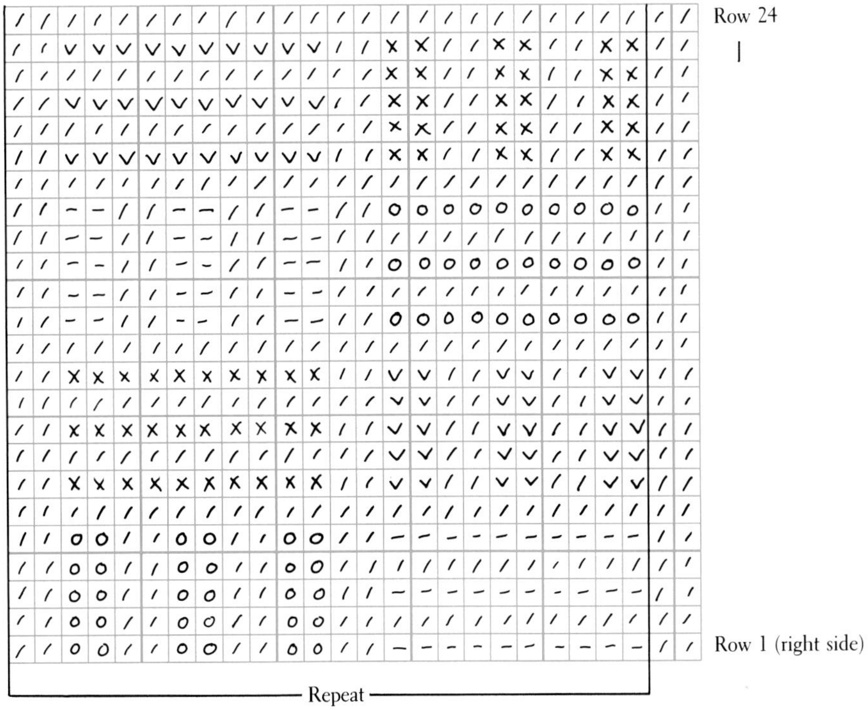

Row 24

Row 1 (right side)

— Repeat —

Each block = 1 stitch and row

/ = MC
— = A
O = B
∨ = C
✗ = D

Bobble Sampler

Experienced

A generously textured and elaborately patterned afghan will enhance any room. Single crochet and triple crochet bobbles are used in this portable project.

SIZE
42″ × 58½″

MATERIALS
Bernat Berella "4" (worsted-weight acrylic) 3½ oz/240
  yd balls: 12 balls Green
Size J/10 crochet hook (or size for gauge)

GAUGE
Each square = 8¼″

SEE
Reverse Slip Stitch, Surface Slip Stitch, and Triple Crochet Bobbles

THE AFGHAN

SQUARE 1 (make 4)
Ch 32.
Row 1: Sc in 2nd ch from hook and each ch across—31 sts
Rows 2–3: Ch 1, turn, sc in first st and each st across.
Refer to Stitch Chart 1.
Row 4 (wrong side): Work Chart Row 4 as follows: Ch 1, turn, sl st in first st, (tr in next st, sl st in next st) 3 times, *sc in next 5 sts, sl st in next st, (tr in next st, sl st in next st) 3 times, repeat from * 1 time more **(tr bobbles formed on right side of work).**
Work Chart Rows 5–35 in same manner; end.

SQUARE 2 (make 5)
Work as for Square 1 through Row 2.
Refer to Stitch Chart 2.

Row 3 (wrong side): Work Chart Row 3 as follows: Ch 1, turn, sc in first st, sl st in next st, (tr in next st, sl st in next st) 2 times, *sc in next 7 sts, sl st in next st, (tr in next st, sl st in next st) 2 times, repeat from * 1 time more, sc in last st **(tr bobbles formed on right side of work).**
Work Chart Rows 4–35 in same manner; end.

SQUARE 3 (make 5)
Work as for Square 1 through Row 3.
Refer to Stitch Chart 3.
Row 4 (wrong side): Work Chart Row 4 as follows: Ch 1, turn, sc in first 2 sts, sl st in next st, tr in next st, sl st in next st, *sc in next 3 sts, sl st in next st, tr in next st, sl st in next st, repeat from * across, sc in last 2 sts **(tr bobbles formed on right side of work).**
Work Chart Rows 5–35 in same manner; end.

SQUARE 4 (make 5)
Work as for Square 1 through Row 3.
Refer to Stitch Chart 4.
Row 4 (wrong side): Work Chart Row 4 as follows: Ch 1, turn, sc in first 14 sts, sl st in next st, tr in next st, sl st in next st, sc in last 14 sts **(tr bobble formed on right side of work).**
Work Chart Rows 5–35 in same manner; end.

SQUARE 5 (make 5)
Work as for Square 1 through Row 3.
Refer to Stitch Chart 5.
Row 4 (wrong side): Work Chart Row 4 as follows: Ch 1, turn, sc in first 8 sts, *sl st in next st, tr in next

BOBBLE SAMPLER STITCH CHART 1

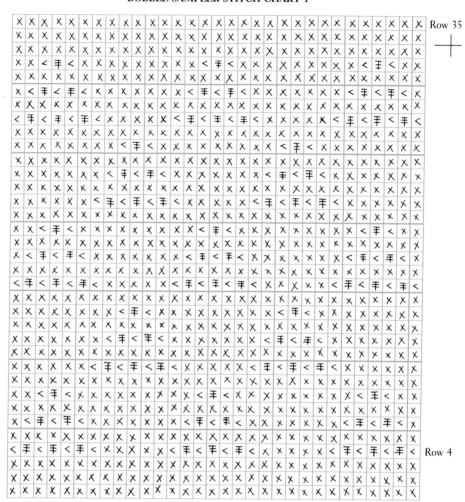

Row 35

Row 4

Each block = 1 stitch and row

$<^*$ = Sl st

$\times^*$ = Sc

$\mathbf{\mp}^*$ = Tr

*International Crochet Symbol

BOBBLE SAMPLER STITCH CHART 2

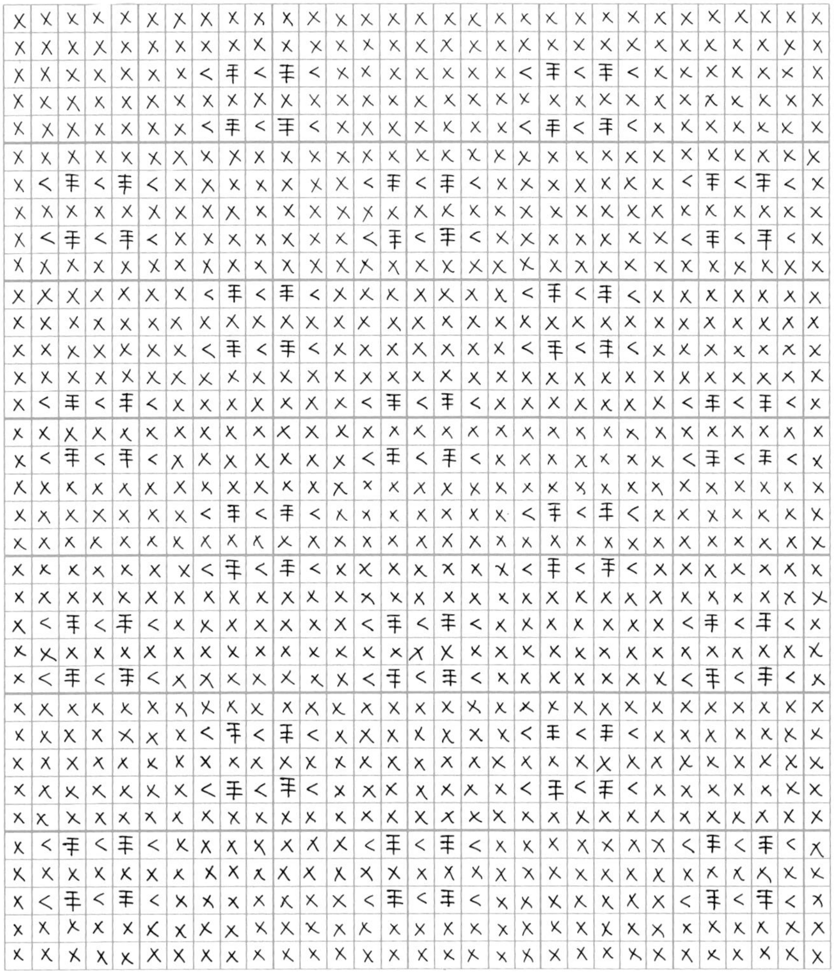

Row 35

Row 3

Each block = 1 stitch and row

$<^*$ = Sl st

$×^*$ = Sc

$\mp^*$ = Tr

*International Crochet Symbol

BOBBLE SAMPLER STITCH CHART 3

Row 35

Row 4

Each block = 1 stitch and row

$<^*$ = Sl st

$\times^*$ = Sc

$\mathbf{\mp}^*$ = Tr

BOBBLE SAMPLER STITCH CHART 4

Row 35

Row 4

Each block = 1 stitch and row

$<^*$ = Sl st

$\times^*$ = Sc

$\mp^*$ = Tr

*International Crochet Symbol

BOBBLE SAMPLER STITCH CHART 5

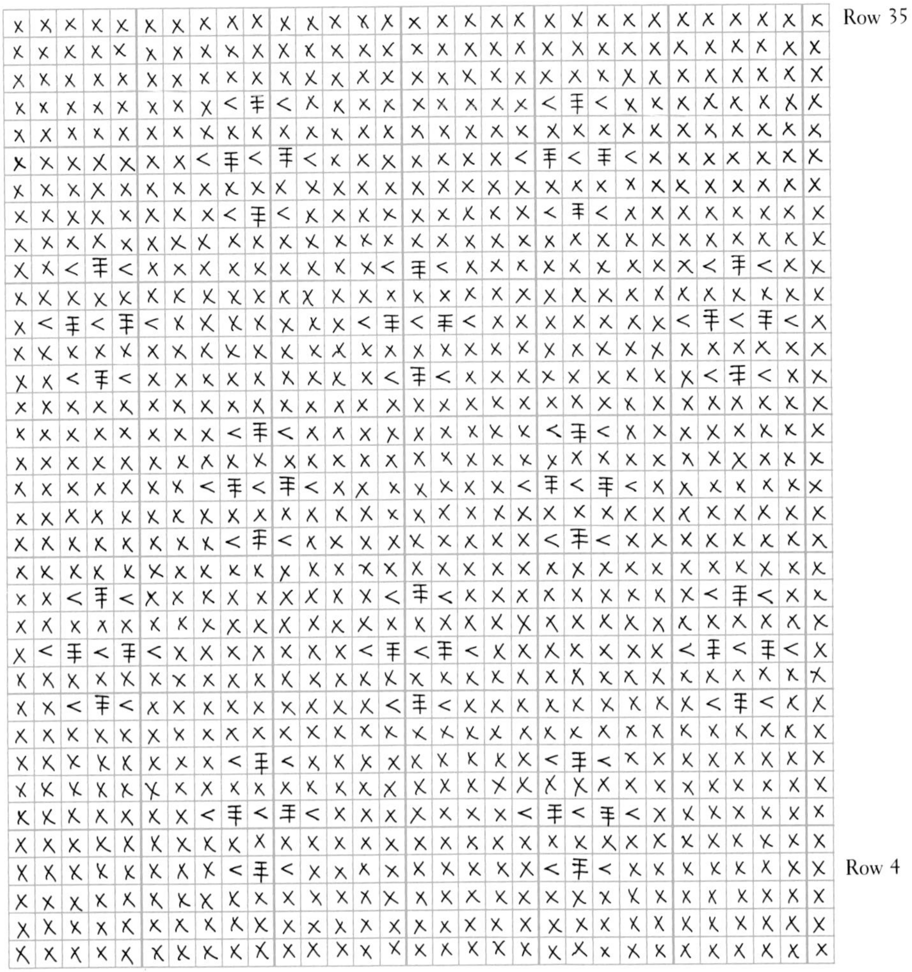

Row 35

Row 4

Each block = 1 stitch and row

$<$* = Sl st

$\times$* = Sc

$\mp$* = Tr

*International Crochet Symbol

96

st, sl st in next st*, sc in next 9 sts, repeat between *s 1 time more, sc in last 8 sts (**tr bobbles formed on right side of work**).
Work Chart Rows 5–35 in same manner; end.

SQUARE 6 (make 4)
Work as for Square 1 through Row 1.
Row 2 (wrong side): Ch 1, turn, sc in first 2 sts, sl st in next st, tr in next st, sl st in next st, *sc in next 3 sts, sl st in next st, tr in next st, sl st in next st, repeat from * across, sc in last 2 sts (**tr bobbles formed on right side of work**).
Row 3: Ch 1, turn, sc in first st and each st across.
Rows 4–35: Repeat Rows 2–3; end.

SQUARE 7 (make 4)
Work as for Square 1 through Row 2.
Row 3 (wrong side): Ch 1, turn, sl st in first st, *tr in next st, sl st in next st, repeat from * across (**tr bobbles formed on right side of work**).
Rows 4–8: Ch 1, turn, sc in first st and each st across.
Row 9: Repeat Row 3.
Rows 10–33: Repeat Rows 4–9.
Rows 34–35: Repeat Row 4; end.

SQUARE 8 (make 3)
Work as for Square 1 through Row 1.
Row 2 (wrong side): Ch 1, turn, sl st in first st, tr in next st, sl st in next st, *sc in next st, sl st in next st, tr in next st, sl st in next st, repeat from * across (**tr bobbles formed on right side of work**).
Row 3: Ch 1, turn, sc in first st and each st across.
Row 4: Ch 1, turn, sc in first 2 sts, *sl st in next st, tr in next st, sl st in next st, sc in next st, repeat from * across, sc in last st.
Row 5: Repeat Row 3.
Rows 6–33: Repeat Rows 2–5.
Rows 34–35: Repeat Rows 2–3; end.

ASSEMBLY
Refer to Assembly Diagram. With right sides facing and overcast stitch, sew squares together following diagram.

BOBBLE SAMPLER ASSEMBLY DIAGRAM

1	2	7	8	4
3	4	5	6	3
2	7	3	4	5
6	5	1	2	7
4	2	6	8	1
3	1	5	6	3
5	7	8	4	2

EDGING
With right side facing, join yarn.
Rnd 1: Work a rnd of sc evenly around entire piece, making 3 sc at each corner; join with sl st to first sc.
Rnd 2: Ch 1, **don't** turn, work a reverse sl st in each st of previous rnd; join with sl st to first reverse sl st.
Rnd 3: Ch 1, **don't** turn, working below previous rnd, work a rnd of surface sl st around posts of sts of Rnd 1; join with sl st to first surface sl st.
Rnd 4: Repeat Rnd 3; end.
Secure and trim loose ends.

Waves

Beginner

*Shh, shh . . . soft waves sing the song of the sea
on a background as white as the sandiest beach.
Single crochet and cross-stitch embroidery
are used in this quick-to-complete project.*

SIZE

48″ × 62″ (before fringe)

MATERIALS

Lion Brand Jiffy (chunky-weight, brushed Orlon) 3 oz/
135 yd balls: 20 balls White (MC); 1 ball each Navy
(A), Turquoise (B), Medium Blue (C), and Aqua (D)
Size K/10½ crochet hook (or size for gauge)
Yarn needle

GAUGE

17 sts = 5″; 25 rows = 6″ (in pattern stitch)

SEE

Cross-stitch Embroidery and Fringe

ONE-PIECE AFGHAN

With MC, ch 163.

Row 1: Sc in 2nd ch from hook and each ch across—
162 sts.

Row 2: Ch 1, turn, sc in first st and each st across.
With MC only, repeat Row 2 until piece measures
61½″ from beginning; end.

EMBROIDERY

The design is worked in cross-stitch embroidery across
the short edge of the afghan. Use the yarn needle and
a single strand of yarn. **Refer to Embroidery Chart.**
Leaving the edge stitch of both sides and the first twelve
rows unembroidered, work the chart, beginning and
repeating as indicated. Repeat on other side.

EDGING

With right side facing and MC, work a rnd of sc evenly
around entire piece, making 3 sc at each corner; join
with sl st to first sc; end.
Secure and trim loose ends.

FRINGE

Cut 12″ lengths of MC. With wrong side facing, using
3 strands together for each fringe, attach fringe at corner and at every 3rd st across short edge of afghan.
Repeat on other side.

WAVES EMBROIDERY CHART

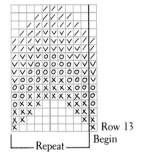

Each block = 1 stitch and row
(count turning ch as 1 st when embroidering)

X = A
O = B
V = C
/ = D

Seashells

Experienced

*Since the dawn of history, mankind has been enchanted
with the beauty of shells. Single crochet,
a single crochet mesh pattern, and cross-stitch embroidery
are used in this portable project.*

SIZE
48½″ × 66″

MATERIALS
Unger Utopia (worsted-weight acrylic), 3½ oz/240 yd
  balls: 6 balls White (A); 7 balls Brown (B); 2 balls
  Peach (C)
Size J/10 crochet hook (or size for gauge)
Yarn needle

GAUGE
Each square = 8¾″

SEE
Cross-stitch Embroidery, Reverse Slip Stitch, Surface
Slip Stitch, and Working with Chain Spaces/Behind

THE AFGHAN

BASIC SQUARE (make 35)
With A, ch 23.
Row 1: Sc in 2nd ch from hook and each ch across—
22 sts.
Rows 2–24: Ch 1, turn, sc in first st and each st across;
end.

EMBROIDERY
The design is worked in cross-stitch embroidery. Use
the yarn needle and a single strand of yarn.

Square 1 (make 9)
Refer to Embroidery Chart 1. Embroider following
chart.

Square 2 (make 14)
Refer to Embroidery Chart 2. Embroider following
chart.

Square 3 (make 12)
Leave remaining squares plain.

SQUARE BORDER
With right side facing, join A.
Rnd 1: Work a rnd of sc around entire square, having
21 sc evenly spaced along each side and making 3 sc
at each corner; join with sl st to first sc; end.
Rnd 2: With right side facing, join B; sc in each st
around, making 3 sc at each corner; join with sl st to
first sc.
Rnd 3: Ch 1, **don't** turn, continuing with B, repeat
Rnd 2; end.
Rnd 4: With right side facing, join C at any corner;
ch 1, *sc in 2nd of 3 corner sc, ch 1, sc in same st,
ch 1, sk next st, (sc in next st, ch 1, sk next st), repeat
between () to corner, repeat from *3 times more, join
with sl st to first sc; end.
Rnd 5: With right side facing, join B in any corner
sp; ch 1, *3 sc in corner sp, sc in next st, (working
behind ch-1 of previous rnd, sc in next skipped st of
that rnd, sc in next st), repeat between () to corner,
repeat from * 3 times more, join with sl st to first sc;
don't end.
Rnd 6: Repeat Rnd 3; end.

SEASHELLS EMBROIDERY CHARTS

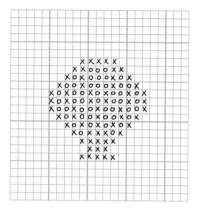

CHART 1

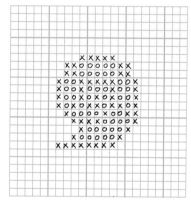

CHART 2

Each block = 1 stitch and row
(count turning ch as 1 st when embroidering)
X = B
O = C

ASSEMBLY
Refer to Assembly Diagram. With right sides facing, B, and overcast st, sew squares together following diagram.

AFGHAN BORDER
With right side facing, join B.

Rnd 1: Work a rnd of sc evenly around entire piece, having an odd number of stitches along each edge and making 3 sc at each corner; join with sl st to first sc.

Rnds 2–5: Work Rnds 3–6 of Square Border around entire outer edge of afghan; **don't** end.

Rnd 6: Ch 1, **don't** turn, work a reverse sl st in each st of previous rnd; join with sl st to first reverse sl st.

Rnd 7: Ch 1, **don't** turn, working below previous rnd, work a rnd of surface sl st around posts of sts of Rnd 5; join with sl st to first surface sl st; end.
Secure and trim loose ends.

SEASHELLS ASSEMBLY DIAGRAM

1	3	2	3	1
3	2	1	2	3
2	3	2	3	2
1	2	1	2	1
2	3	2	3	2
3	2	1	2	3
1	3	2	3	1

City
Chic

Flying Geese

Intermediate

*Color it city bright, and this version of a
beloved quilt is a contemporary complement.
Diagonal color-change granny squares
are used in this portable project.*

SIZE
47" × 62"

MATERIALS
Reynolds Reynelle Deluxe (worsted-weight acrylic),
   3½ oz/240 yd balls: 6 balls Black (A); 3 balls Red
   (B); 4 balls Gray (C)
Size H/8 crochet hook (or size for gauge)

GAUGE
Each square = 2½"

SEE
Changing Color, Reverse Slip Stitch, and Working in
Rounds

NOTE
Joining slip stitch counts as last chain of round.

THE AFGHAN

BASIC SQUARE
With first color, ch 4; join with sl st to form ring.
Rnd 1 (right side): Ch 3 (first dc), 2 dc in ring, ch 2,
3 dc in ring, ch 1; with **second color** (**don't** end first
color), ch 1, 3 dc in ring, ch 2, 3 dc in ring, ch 1;
join with sl st to top of ch-3; **don't** end.
Rnd 2: Continuing with second color, ch 1, **turn**, sl
st in corner sp just completed, ch 3 (first dc), 2 dc in
sp, *ch 1, 3 dc in next sp, ch 2, 3 dc in same sp, ch

1, 3 dc in next sp, ch 1*; with **first color**, ch 1 (end
second color), 3 dc in same sp, repeat between *s; join
with sl st to top of ch-3; end.

SQUARE 1
Make 96 squares using B for first color and A for second
color.

SQUARE 2
Make 160 squares using C for first color and A for
second color.

SQUARE 3
Make 66 squares using B for first color and C for second
color.

STRIP 1 (make 4)

Assembly
Refer to Strip 1 Assembly Diagram. Work diagram
from X *to* Y, then repeat from Y *to* Z 11 times. With
right sides facing, corresponding color, and sl st, catching outer lps only, crochet squares together to form
horizontal pairs. Join horizontal pairs into strip in same
manner. Work edging to complete strip.

Edging
With right side facing, join A in any corner sp.
Rnd 1: Ch 3 (first dc), 2 dc in sp, ch 2, 3 dc in same
sp, (ch 1, 3 dc) repeat between () into each sp and
joining to corner, *ch 1, 3 dc in corner sp, ch 2, 3

FLYING GEESE STRIP ASSEMBLY DIAGRAMS

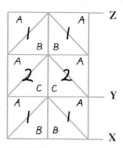

STRIP 1

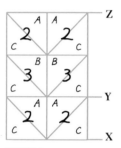

STRIP 2

Two-color square orientation is indicated by diagonal line and color codes in corners.

dc in same sp, repeat between () into each sp and joining to corner, repeat from * 2 times more; join with sl st to top of ch-3; end.

STRIP 2 (make 3)
Work as for Strip 1 but use **Strip 2 Assembly Diagram** and work edging with B.

AFGHAN ASSEMBLY
Arrange strips alternately, beginning and ending with Strip 1. Crochet strips together in same manner as for squares.

AFGHAN EDGING
With right side facing, join A in any corner sp.
Rnd 1: Work Rnd 1 of Strip Edging around entire outer edge of afghan; **don't** end.
Rnd 2: Sl st to corner sp, 2 sl st in sp, ch 3 (first dc), **turn**, 2 dc in sp, ch 2, 3 dc in same sp, (ch 1, 3 dc in next sp), repeat between () to corner, *ch 1, 3 dc in corner sp, ch 2, 3 dc in same sp, repeat between () to corner, repeat from * 2 times more; join with sl st to top of ch-3.
Rnd 3: Ch 1, **turn**, sc in each st and sp around, making 3 sc in each corner sp; join with sl st to first sc.
Rnd 4: Ch 1, **don't** turn, work a reverse sl st in each st of previous rnd; join with sl st to first reverse sl st; end.

Secure and trim loose ends.

On Target
Beginner

*Bull's eye! High-contrast colors and a diamond
pattern win for masculine settings.
Basic granny squares, arranged on the diagonal,
are used in this portable project.*

SIZE
55" × 66½"

MATERIALS
Unger Utopia (worsted-weight acrylic), 3½ oz/240 yd
   balls: 6 balls Black (MC); 4 balls each White (A)
   and Green (B)
Size H/8 crochet hook (or size for gauge)

GAUGE
Each square = 4⅝"

SEE
Reverse Slip Stitch and Working in Rounds

NOTE
Joining slip stitch counts as last chain of round.

THE AFGHAN

SQUARE 1 (make 80)
With A, ch 4; join with sl st to form ring.
Rnd 1 (right side): Ch 3 (first dc), 2 dc in ring, (ch
2, 3 dc in ring) 3 times, ch 1; join with sl st to top of
ch-3.
Rnd 2: Sl st to next sp; ch 3 (first dc), **don't** turn, 2
dc in sp, ch 2, 3 dc in same sp, (ch 1, 3 dc in next
sp, ch 2, 3 dc in same sp) 3 times; join with sl st to
top of ch-3; end.
Rnd 3: With right side facing, join B in any corner
sp; ch 3 (first dc), **don't** turn, 2 dc in sp, ch 2, 3 dc

in same sp, ch 1, 3 dc in next sp, (ch 1, 3 dc in next
sp, ch 2, 3 dc in same sp, ch 1, 3 dc in next sp) 3
times; join with sl st to top of ch-3; end.
Rnd 4: With MC, work as for Rnd 3, making 1 more
3-dc group per side; end.

SQUARE 2 (make 63)
Work as for Square 1, **but** use B where A is called for
and A where B is called for.

HALF-SQUARE 3 (make 18)
With B, ch 4; join with sl st to form ring.
Rnd 1: Ch 4 (first dc, ch 1), 3 dc in ring, ch 2, 3 dc
in ring, ch 1, dc in ring; end.
Rnd 2: Join B in first ch-1 sp; ch 4 (first dc, ch 1),
don't turn, 3 dc in same sp, ch 1, 3 dc in next sp, ch
2, 3 dc in same sp (**corner made**), ch 1, 3 dc in last
sp, ch 1, dc in same sp; end.
Rnd 3: Join A in first ch-1 sp; ch 4 (first dc, ch 1),
don't turn, 3 dc in same sp, (ch 1, 3 dc in next sp) 2
times, ch 2, 3 dc in same sp, (ch 1, 3 dc in next sp)
2 times, ch 1, dc in same sp; end.
Rnd 4: With MC, work as for Rnd 3, making 1 more
3-dc group per side; end.

ASSEMBLY
Refer to Assembly Diagram. With right sides facing,
MC, and sl st, catching outer lps only, crochet squares
together to form diagonal strips, as indicated by shading on diagram. Join diagonal strips in same manner.

ON TARGET ASSEMBLY DIAGRAM

Shading indicates diagonal strip orientation.

EDGING

With right side facing, join MC at upper left corner joining.

Rnd 1: Ch 1, *3 sc in corner joining, 2 sc in each sp and joining across long edge to corner, 3 sc in corner joining, (sc in each ch-1 sp and dc to point, 3 sc in ch-2 sp at point, sc in each ch-1 sp and dc to V, at V work sc 3 tog over ch-1 sp, joining, and ch-1 sp), repeat between () across short edge to corner, repeat from * 1 time more; join with sl st to first sc.

Rnd 2: Ch 1, **don't** turn, work a reverse sl st in each st of previous rnd; join with sl st to first reverse sl st; end.

Secure and trim loose ends.

Serape Stripe
Beginner

Ole! Add south-of-the-border sizzle to a room with the vibrant colors of this Mexican-inspired blanket. A single crochet mesh pattern is used in this project.

SIZE
48″ × 68½″ (before fringe)

MATERIALS
Unger Utopia (worsted-weight acrylic), 3½ oz/240 yd balls: 5 balls Black (MC); 2 balls Teal (A); 3 balls Green (B); 2 balls Hot Pink (C); 3 balls Dark Coral (D); 2 balls each Turquoise (E) and Medium Coral (F)

Size J/10 crochet hook (or size for gauge)

GAUGE
17 sts = 4″; 16 rows = 4″ (in pattern stitch)

SEE
Changing Color/End of Row, Fringe, and Working with Chain Spaces/In

NOTE
Afghan is worked from side to side rather than from top to bottom.

STRIPE PATTERN
2 rows A, 2 rows B, 1 row MC, 2 rows C, 2 rows D, 2 rows MC, 2 rows B, 2 rows E, 1 row MC, 2 rows D, 2 rows F, 2 rows MC

ONE-PIECE AFGHAN

With MC, ch 290.
Row 1: Sc in 2nd ch from hook and each ch across—289 sts.

Row 2: Ch 1, turn, sc in first st, *ch 1, sk next st, sc in next st, repeat from * across; end.
Join A.
Begin stripe pattern next row.
Row 3: Ch 1, turn, sc in first st, sc in first ch-1 sp, *ch 1, sk next st, sc in next ch-1 sp, repeat from * across, sc in last st.
Row 4: Ch 1, turn, sc in first st, *ch 1, sk next st, sc in next ch-1 sp, repeat from * across, end with sc in last st (rather than ch-1 sp).
Repeating Rows 3–4 throughout, continue with stripe pattern.
Repeat the 22 stripe-pattern rows 7 times more, then repeat the first 11 rows 1 time; end.

EDGING
With right side facing and MC, work a rnd of sc evenly around entire piece, making 3 sc at each corner; join with sl st to first sc; end.
Secure and trim loose ends.

FRINGE
Cut 12″ lengths of MC. With wrong side facing, using 3 strands together for each fringe, attach fringe at corner and at every 3rd st across short edge of afghan. Repeat on other side.

Castle Walls

Experienced

*The accent's on drama as a classic quilt pattern
comes boldly and brightly to crochet. Basic and
diagonal color-change granny squares
are used in this portable project.*

SIZE
64″ × 64″

MATERIALS
Unger Utopia (worsted-weight acrylic), 3½ oz/240 yd
   balls: 8 balls each Black (A) and Blue (B); 2 balls
   Turquoise (C); 1 ball Green (D)
Size H/8 crochet hook (or size for gauge)

GAUGE
Each square = 2⅝″

SEE
Changing Color, Reverse Slip Stitch, and Working in
Rounds

NOTE
Joining slip stitch counts as last chain of round.

THE AFGHAN

SOLID-COLOR SQUARE
Ch 4; join with sl st to form ring.
Rnd 1 (right side): Ch 3 (first dc), 2 dc in ring, (ch
1, 3 dc in ring) 3 times, ch 1; join with sl st to top of
ch-3.
Rnd 2: Ch 3 (first dc), **turn,** 2 dc in sp, ch 2, 3 dc in
same sp, (ch 1, 3 dc in next sp, ch 2, 3 dc in same
sp) 3 times; join with sl st to top of ch-3; end.

TWO-COLOR SQUARE
With first color, ch 4; join with sl st to form ring.

Rnd 1 (right side): Ch 3 (first dc), 2 dc in ring, ch 2,
3 dc in ring, ch 1; with **second color** (**don't** end first
color), ch 1, 3 dc in ring, ch 2, 3 dc in ring, ch 1;
join with sl st to top of ch-3; **don't** end.
Rnd 2: Continuing with second color, ch 1, **turn,** sl
st in corner sp just completed, ch 3 (first dc), 2 dc in
sp, *ch 1, 3 dc in next sp, ch 2, 3 dc in same sp, ch
1, 3 dc in next sp, ch 1*; with **first color,** ch 1 (end
second color), 3 dc in same sp, repeat between *s; join
with sl st to top of ch-3; end.

SQUARE 1
Make **76** solid-color squares with A.

SQUARE 2
Make **41** solid-color squares with B.

SQUARE 3
Make **16** solid-color squares with C.

SQUARE 4
Make **24** two-color squares using B for first color and
A for second color.

SQUARE 5
Make **12** two-color squares using C for first color and
A for second color.

SQUARE 6
Make **16** two-color squares using B for first color and
D for second color.

CASTLE WALLS ASSEMBLY DIAGRAM

1	1	1	4	2	6	2	2	2	6	2	4	1	1	1
1	1	4	2	8	7	3	3	3	7	8	2	4	1	1
1	4	2	8	5	1	1	1	1	1	5	8	2	4	1
4	2	8	5	1	1	1	1	1	1	5	8	2	4	
2	8	5	1	1	4	6	2	6	4	1	1	5	8	2
6	7	1	1	4	8	7	3	7	8	4	1	1	7	6
2	3	1	1	6	7	8	2	8	7	6	1	1	3	2
2	3	1	1	2	3	2	2	2	3	2	1	1	3	2
2	3	1	1	6	7	8	2	8	7	6	1	1	3	2
6	7	1	1	4	8	7	3	7	8	4	1	1	7	6
2	8	5	1	1	4	6	2	6	4	1	1	5	8	2
4	2	8	5	1	1	1	1	1	1	5	8	2	4	
1	4	2	8	5	1	1	1	1	1	5	8	2	4	1
1	1	4	2	8	7	3	3	3	7	8	2	4	1	1
1	1	1	4	2	6	2	2	2	6	2	4	1	1	1

Two-color square orientation is indicated by diagonal line and color codes in corners.

SQUARE 7

Make 16 two-color squares using C for first color and D for second color.

SQUARE 8

Make 24 two-color squares using C for first color and B for second color.

ASSEMBLY

Refer to Assembly Diagram. With right sides facing, corresponding color, and sl st, catching outer lps only, crochet squares together to form vertical strips. Join vertical strips in same manner.

BORDER

With right side facing, join A in any corner sp.

Rnd 1: Ch 3 (first dc), 2 dc in sp, ch 2, 3 dc in same sp, (ch 1, 3 dc), repeat between () into each sp and joining to corner, *ch 1, 3 dc in corner sp, ch 2, 3 dc in same sp, repeat between () into each sp and joining to corner, repeat from * 2 times more; join with sl st to top of ch-3.

Rnds 2–12: Sl st to corner sp, 2 sl st in sp, ch 3 (first dc), **turn,** 2 dc in sp, ch 2, 3 dc in same sp, (ch 1, 3 dc in next sp), repeat between () to corner, *ch 1, 3 dc in corner sp, ch 2, 3 dc in same sp, repeat between () to corner, repeat from * 2 times more; join with sl st to top of ch-3; end after Rnd 12.

Rnd 13: With wrong side facing, join B in any corner sp; work as for Rnd 2, beginning with ch-3.

Rnds 14–24: Repeat Rnd 2; **don't** end.

Rnd 25: Ch 1, **turn,** sc in each st and sp around, making 3 sc in each corner sp; join with sl st to first sc.

Rnd 26: Ch 1, **don't** turn, work a reverse sl st in each st of previous rnd; join with sl st to first reverse sl st; end.

Secure and trim loose ends.

Ripple
Experienced

A perennial crochet favorite goes modern!
A single crochet mesh pattern is used in this project.

SIZE
52½" × 62½"

MATERIALS
Unger Utopia (worsted-weight acrylic) 3½ oz/240 yd balls: 6 balls Teal (A); 3 balls each Turquoise (B), Aqua (C), and White (D)
Size J/10 crochet hook (or size for gauge)

GAUGE
16 sts = 3"; 9 rows = 3" (in pattern stitch)

SEE
Changing Color/End of Row, Increasing, Decreasing, Reverse Slip Stitch, and Working with Chain Spaces/In

STRIPE PATTERN
1 row B, 1 row A, 2 rows C, 1 row D, 2 rows C, 1 row A, 1 row B, 2 rows A, 1 row C, 1 row A, 2 rows D, 1 row B, 2 rows D, 1 row A, 1 row C, 2 rows A, 1 row D, 1 row A, 2 rows B, 1 row A, 2 rows B, 1 row A, 1 row D, 2 rows A

ONE-PIECE AFGHAN
With A, ch 280.
Row 1: Sc in 2nd ch from hook, sc in next ch, sk next ch, sc in next 11 chs, 3 sc in next ch (point inc of 2 made), sc in next 11 chs, *sk next 2 chs (V dec of 2 made), sc in next 11 chs, 3 sc in next ch (point inc of 2 made), sc in next 11 chs, repeat from * 9 times more, end with sk next ch, sc in last 2 chs.
Row 2: Ch 1, turn, sc in first 2 sts, sk next st, sc in next st, (ch 1, sk next st, sc in next st) 5 times, ch 1, sc in next st, ch 1 (point inc of 2 made), sc in next st, (ch 1, sk next st, sc in next st) 5 times, *sk next 2 sts (V dec of 2 made), sc in next st, (ch 1, sk next st, sc in next st) 5 times, ch 1, sc in next st, ch 1 (point inc of 2 made), sc in next st, (ch 1, sk next st, sc in next st) 5 times, repeat from * 9 times more, end with sk next st, sc in last 2 sts.
Row 3: Ch 1, turn, sc in first 2 sts, sk next st, sc in next ch-1 sp, (ch 1, sk next st, sc in next ch-1 sp) 5 times, ch 1, sc in next st, ch 1 (point inc of 2 made), sc in next ch-1 sp, (ch 1, sk next st, sc in next ch-1 sp) 5 times, *sk next 2 sts (V dec of 2 made), sc in next ch-1 sp, (ch 1, sk next st, sc in next ch-1 sp) 5 times, ch 1, sc in next st, ch 1 (point inc of 2 made), sc in next ch-1 sp, (ch 1, sk next st, sc in next ch-1 sp) 5 times, repeat from * 9 times more, end with sk next st, sc in last 2 sts.
Repeat Row 3 throughout.
Begin stripe pattern next row.
Work the 33 stripe-pattern rows 5 times, then work the first 11 stripe-pattern rows 1 time more. Continue with A for one row more; end.

EDGING
With right side facing, join A.
Rnd 1: Work a rnd of sc evenly around entire piece, making 3 sc at each point (inc), and skipping 2 sc at each V (dec); join with sl st to first sc.
Rnd 2: Ch 1, **don't** turn, work a reverse sl st in each st of previous rnd; join with sl st to first reverse sl st; end. Secure and trim loose ends.

Diagonal Dash

Intermediate

*This sophisticated geometric design would be
a handsome addition to a man's room.
Double crochet carried-thread color work
is used in this quick-to-complete project.*

SIZE
50" × 52"

MATERIALS
Bernat Berella "4" (worsted-weight acrylic) 3½ oz/240
 yd balls: 4 balls each Gray (A) and Natural (B); 1
 ball Red (C); 2 balls Brown (D); 1 ball Gold (E)
Size H/8 crochet hook (or size for gauge)

GAUGE
18 sts = 5"; 9 rows = 5" (in pattern stitch)

SEE
Changing Color/Within a Row and Reverse Slip Stitch

ONE-PIECE AFGHAN

With A, ch 178.
Base Row: Dc in 4th ch from hook and each ch
across—176 sts.
Refer to Stitch Chart.
Row 1 (right side): Work Chart Row 1 from **right to
left** as follows: With A, ch 3 (first dc), turn, sk first st,
dc in next st; with C, dc in next 2 sts; (with A, dc in
next 10 sts; with C, dc in next 2 sts) 14 times; with A,
dc in last 4 sts.
Row 2: Work Chart Row 2 from **left to right** as follows:
With A, ch 3 (first dc), turn, sk first st, dc in next 3
sts; with C, dc in next 2 sts; (with A, dc in next 10 sts;
with C, dc in next 2 sts) 14 times; with A, dc in last
2 sts.
Work Chart Rows 3–91 in same manner; end.

EDGING
With right side facing, join D.
Rnd 1: Work a rnd of sc evenly around entire piece,
making 3 sc at each corner; join with sl st to first sc.
Rnd 2: Ch 2 (first hdc), **don't** turn, sk first st, hdc in
each st around, making 3 hdc at each corner; join with
sl st to top of ch-2.
Rnd 3: Ch 1, **don't** turn, work a reverse sl st in each
st of previous rnd; join with sl st to first reverse sl st;
end.
Secure and trim loose ends.

Each block = 1 stitch and row   / = A   ☐ = B   ✗ = C   ○ = D   ∨ = E

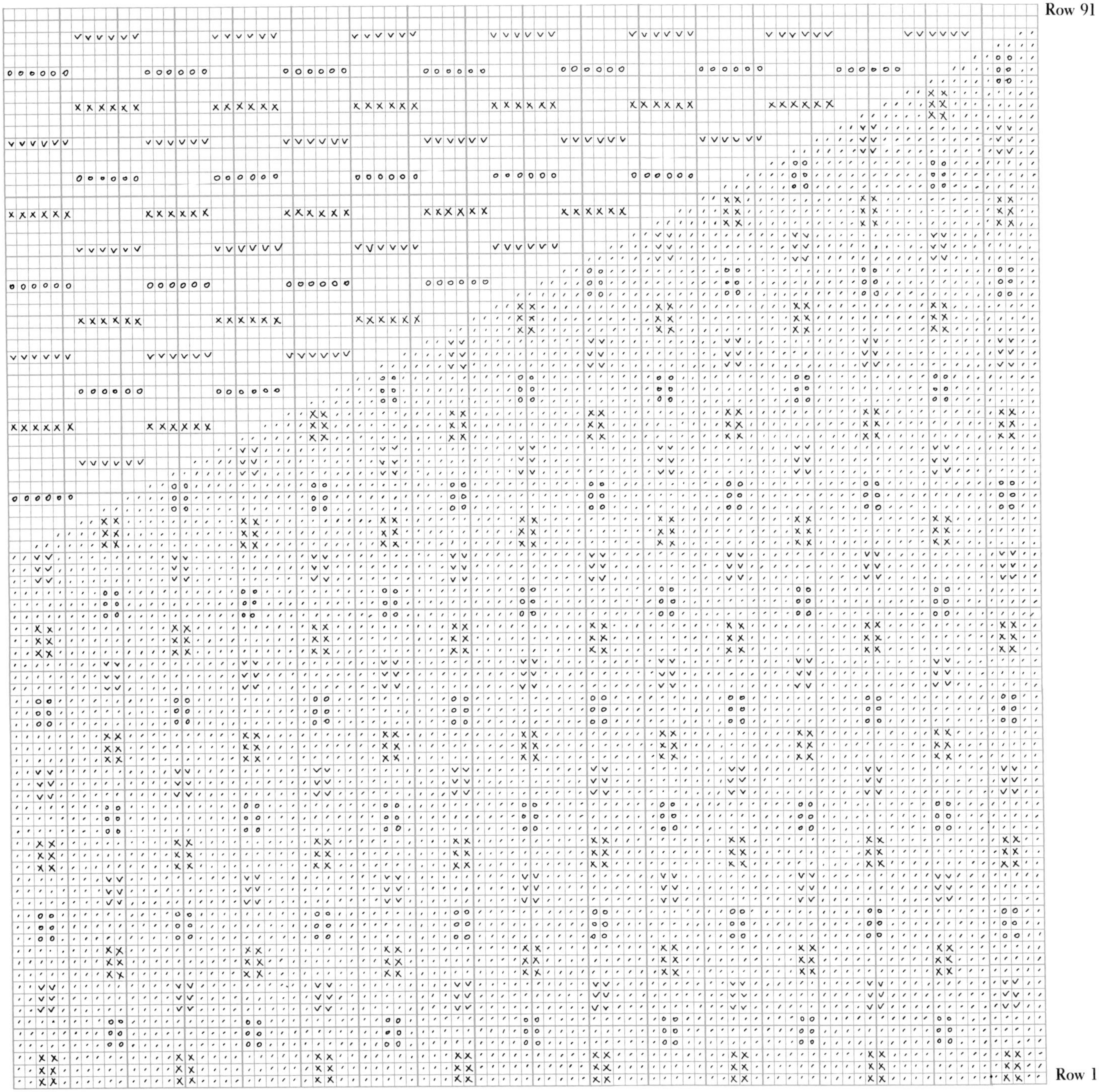
Row 91
Row 1

Lightning
Intermediate

*This striking afghan combines native design
with patriotic colors for a style that's distinctly American.
Double crochet carried-thread color work
is used in this quick-to-complete project.*

SIZE
47″ × 65½″

MATERIALS
Bernat Berella "4" (worsted-weight acrylic) 3½ oz/240
  yd balls: 9 balls Blue (MC); 1 ball Rose (A); 2 balls
  White (B)
Size H/8 crochet hook (or size for gauge)

GAUGE
14 sts = 4″; 13 rows = 7″ (in pattern stitch)

SEE
Changing Color and Reverse Slip Stitch

ONE-PIECE AFGHAN

With MC, ch 164.
Base Row: Dc in 4th ch from hook and each ch
across—162 sts.
Next Row: Ch 3 (first dc), turn, sk first st, dc in each
st across.
Repeat the last row 1 time more.
Refer to Stitch Chart.
Row 1 (right side): Work Chart Row 1 from **right** to
left as follows: With MC, ch 3 (first dc), turn, sk first

st, dc in next 7 sts; with A, dc in next 2 sts; (with MC,
dc in next 14 sts; with A, dc in next 2 sts) 9 times;
with MC, dc in last 8 sts.
Row 2: Work Chart Row 2 from **left to right** as follows:
With MC, ch 3 (first dc), turn, sk first st, dc in next
5 sts; with A, dc in next 2 sts; (with B, dc in next 2
sts; with A, dc in next 2 sts; with MC, dc in next 10
sts; with A, dc in next 2 sts) 9 times; with B, dc in
next 2 sts; with A, dc in next 2 sts; with MC, dc in
last 6 sts.
Work Chart Rows 3–20 in same manner.
With MC only, work in dc until piece measures 52½″
from beginning, ending with right-side row.
Work Chart Rows 1–20 in **reverse** order (begin with
Row 20 and end with Row 1).
With MC only, work in dc for 3 rows; end.

EDGING
With right side facing, join MC.
Rnd 1: Work a rnd of sc evenly around entire piece,
making 3 sc at each corner; join with sl st to first sc.
Rnd 2: Ch 1, **don't** turn, work a reverse sl st in each
st of previous rnd; join with sl st to first reverse sl st;
end.
Secure and trim loose ends.

LIGHTNING STITCH CHART

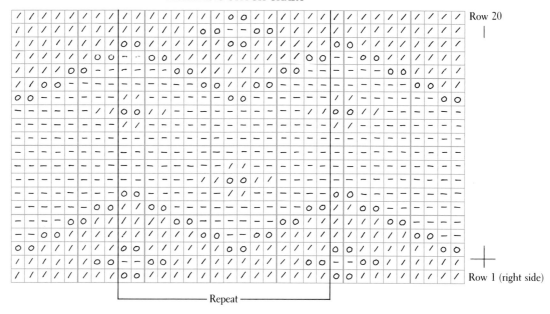

Row 20

Row 1 (right side)

—— Repeat ——

Each block = 1 stitch and row

/ = MC

O = A

— = B

Youthfully
Bright

Tulips

Intermediate

*Pastel flowers and a winsome rickrack pattern
will add a breath of spring to a little girl's room.
Single crochet, a single crochet mesh pattern, and cross-stitch
embroidery are used in this portable project.*

SIZE
48" × 48"

MATERIALS
Unger Utopia (worsted-weight acrylic), 3½ oz/240 yd
balls: 8 balls White (A); 2 balls each Pink (B) and
Peach (C); 1 ball Green (D)
Size J/10 crochet hook (or size for gauge)
Yarn needle

GAUGE
Each square = 6¾"

SEE
Cross-stitch Embroidery, Reverse Slip Stitch, Surface
Slip Stitch, and Working with Chain Spaces/In

THE AFGHAN

BASIC SQUARE (make 24)
With A, ch 25.
Row 1: Sc in 2nd ch from hook and each ch across—
24 sts.
Rows 2–29: Ch 1, turn, sc in first st and each st across;
end.

EMBROIDERY
The design is worked in cross-stitch embroidery. Use
the yarn needle and a single strand of yarn.

SQUARE 1 (make 8)
Refer to Embroidery Chart. Using color B for tulip,
embroider following chart.

SQUARE 2 (make 6)
Refer to Embroidery Chart. Using color C for tulip,
embroider following chart.

TULIPS EMBROIDERY CHART

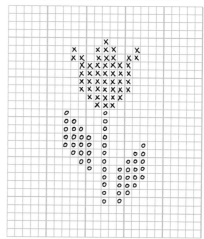

Each block = 1 stitch and row
(count turning ch as 1 st when embroidering)
× = B or C as required
○ = D

126

SQUARE 3 (make 10)
Leave remaining squares plain.

SQUARE 4 (make 25)

Stripe Pattern
2 rows C, 2 rows A, 2 rows B, 2 rows A

With A, ch 30
Row 1: Sc in 2nd ch from hook, *ch 1, sk next ch, sc in next ch, repeat from * across—29 sts (count includes each sc **and** ch-1 sp).
Row 2: With B, ch 1, turn, sc in first st, sc in first ch-1 sp, *ch 1, sk next st, sc in next ch-1 sp, repeat from * across, sc in last st.
Row 3: Ch 1, turn, sc in first st, *ch 1, sk next st, sc in next ch-1 sp, repeat from * across, end with sc in last st (rather than ch-1 sp).
Rows 4–5: With A, repeat Rows 2–3.

Begin stripe pattern next row.
Rows 6–29: Repeating Rows 2–3 throughout, work the 8 stripe-pattern rows 3 times; end.

ASSEMBLY
Refer to Assembly Diagram. With right sides facing, A, and overcast st, sew squares together following diagram.

EDGING
With right side facing, join B.
Rnd 1: Work a rnd of sc evenly around entire piece, making 3 sc at each corner; join with sl st to first sc.
Rnd 2: Ch 1, **don't** turn, work a reverse sl st in each st of previous rnd; join with sl st to first reverse sl st.
Rnd 3: Ch 1, **don't** turn, working below previous rnd, work a rnd of surface sl st around posts of sts of Rnd 1; join with sl st to first surface sl st; end.
Secure and trim loose ends.

TULIPS ASSEMBLY DIAGRAM

4	3	4	1	4	3	4
1	4	3	4	3	4	1
4	2	4	2	4	2	4
3	4	1	4	1	4	3
4	2	4	2	4	2	4
1	4	3	4	3	4	1
4	3	4	1	4	3	4

Pinwheels

Intermediate

A timeless pattern and a favorite toy
make for an afghan every child will enjoy.
Diagonal color-change granny squares
are used in this portable project.

SIZE
45″ × 60″

MATERIALS
Brunswick Fore'n Aft (sport-weight acrylic), 1¾ oz/
  175 yd balls: 8 balls Blue (MC); 2 balls Green (A);
  1 ball each Orange (B) and Yellow (C); 2 balls Pink
  (D)
Size F/5 crochet hook (or size for gauge)

GAUGE
Each square = 4½″

SEE
Changing Color, Reverse Slip Stitch, and Working in
Rounds

NOTE
Joining slip stitch counts as last chain of round.

THE AFGHAN

SQUARE 1 (make 24)
With MC, ch 4; join with sl st to form ring.
Rnd 1 (right side): Ch 3 (first dc), 2 dc in ring, ch 2,
3 dc in ring, ch 1; with **A** (**don't** end MC), ch 1, 3
dc in ring, ch 2, 3 dc in ring, ch 1; join with sl st to
top of ch-3; **don't** end.
Rnd 2: Continuing with A, ch 1, **turn**, sl st in corner
sp just completed, ch 3 (first dc), 2 dc in sp, *ch 1,
3 dc in next sp, ch 2, 3 dc in same sp, ch 1, 3 dc in

next sp, ch 1*; with **MC**, ch 1 (end A), 3 dc in same
sp, repeat between *s; join with sl st to top of ch-3;
don't end.
Rnd 3: Continuing with MC, ch 1, **turn,** sl st in corner
sp just completed, ch 3 (first dc), 2 dc in sp, *(ch 1,
3 dc in next sp) 2 times, ch 2, 3 dc in same sp, repeat
between () 2 times more, ch 1*; with **B** (**don't** end
MC), ch 1, 3 dc in same sp, repeat between *s; join
with sl st to top of ch 3; end B.
Rnd 4: Join C in corner sp just completed; ch 3 (first
dc), **turn,** 2 dc in sp, *(ch 1, 3 dc in next sp) 3 times,
ch 2, 3 dc in same sp, repeat between () 3 times more,
ch 1*; with **MC**, ch 1 (end C), 3 dc in same sp, repeat
between *s; join with sl to top of ch-3; **don't** end.
Rnd 5: Continuing with MC, ch 1, **turn,** sl st in corner
sp just completed, ch 3 (first dc), 2 dc in sp, *(ch 1,
3 dc in next sp) 4 times, ch 2, 3 dc in same sp, repeat
between () 4 times more, ch 1*, with **D**, ch 1 (end
MC), 3 dc in same sp, repeat between *s; join with sl
st to top of ch-3; end.

SQUARE 2 (make 24)
Work as for Square 1 **but** use colors in reverse order
(begin with D for Rnd 1 and end with A for Rnd 5).

BLOCK ASSEMBLY
Refer to Assembly Diagram. Shading indicates areas
crocheted with MC. With right sides facing, MC, and
sl st, catching outer lps only, crochet squares together
to form blocks.

BLOCK BORDER

With right side facing, join MC in any corner sp.

Rnd 1: Ch 3 (first dc), 2 dc in sp, ch 2, 3 dc in same sp, (ch 1, 3 dc), repeat between () into each sp and joining to corner, *ch 1, 3 dc in corner sp, ch 2, 3 dc in same sp, repeat between () into each sp and joining to corner, repeat from * 2 times more; join with sl st to top of ch-3.

Rnd 2: Sl st to corner sp, 2 sl st in sp, ch 3 (first dc), **turn,** 2 dc in sp, ch 2, 3 dc in same sp, (ch 1, 3 dc in next sp), repeat between () to corner, *ch 1, 3 dc in corner sp, ch 2, 3 dc in same sp, repeat between () to corner, repeat from * 2 times more; join with sl st to top of ch-3; end.

Rnd 3: With wrong side facing, join D in any corner sp; work as for Rnd 2, beginning with ch-3; end.

Rnd 4: With right side facing and A, work as for Rnd 3.

Rnd 5: With MC, repeat Rnd 3; **don't** end.

Rnd 6: Continuing with MC, repeat Rnd 2; end.

AFGHAN ASSEMBLY

Crochet blocks together, in same manner as for squares, to form four 3-block rows.

AFGHAN EDGING

With right side facing, join MC in any corner sp.

Rnds 1–2: Work Rnds 1–2 of Block Border around entire outer edge of afghan; **don't** end.

Rnd 3: Ch 1, **turn,** sc in each st and sp around, making 3 sc in each corner sp; join with sl st to first sc.

Rnd 4: Ch 1, **don't** turn, work a reverse sl st in each st of previous rnd; join with sl st to first reverse sl st; end.

Secure and trim loose ends.

PINWHEELS ASSEMBLY DIAGRAM

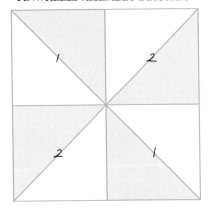

Shading indicates areas crocheted with MC.

Balloon Bright

Beginner

Oops . . . someone's let go of his colorful balloons
and now they're floating off into the summer sky!
Double crochet carried-thread color work is used
in this quick-to-complete, portable project.

SIZE
39″ × 54″

MATERIALS
Coats & Clark Red Heart Classic (worsted-weight Orlon acrylic) 3½ oz/210 yd skeins: 9 skeins Turquoise (MC); 1 skein each Red (A), Yellow (B), and Royal (C)

Size H/8 crochet hook (or size for gauge)

GAUGE
Each square = 7½″

SEE
Changing Color and Reverse Slip Stitch

THE AFGHAN

SQUARE 1 (make 21)
With MC, ch 28.

Row 1 (wrong side): Dc in 4th ch from hook and each ch across—26 sts.

Rows 2–15: Ch 3 (first dc), turn, sk first st, dc in each st across; end.

SQUARE 2 (make 14)
Work as for Square 1 through Row 3.

Refer to Stitch Chart.

Row 4: Work Chart Row 4 as follows: With MC, ch 3 (first dc), turn, sk first st, dc in next 7 sts; with A, dc in 10 sts; with MC, dc in last 8 sts.

Work Chart Rows 5–15 in same manner; end.

BALLOON BRIGHT STITCH CHART

Each block = 1 stitch and row

☐ = MC
× = A
o = B
∨ = C

Row 15

Row 4

ASSEMBLY

Refer to Assembly Diagram. With right sides facing, MC, and overcast st, sew squares together following diagram.

EDGING

With right side facing, join MC.

Rnd 1: Work a rnd of sc evenly around entire piece, making 3 sc at each corner; join with sl st to first sc.

Rnd 2: Ch 2 (first hdc), **don't** turn, sk first st, hdc in each st around, making 3 hdc at each corner; join with sl st to top of ch-2.

Rnd 3: Ch 1, **don't** turn, work a reverse sl st in each st of previous rnd; join with sl st to first reverse sl st; end.

Secure and trim loose ends.

BALLOON BRIGHT ASSEMBLY DIAGRAM

1	1	2	1	1
1	2	1	2	1
2	1	2	1	2
1	2	1	2	1
2	1	2	1	2
1	2	1	2	1
1	1	2	1	1

Baby Floral

Intermediate

*This dainty, carriage-sized blanket would make
a wonderful gift for the new arrival in your life.
A granny square variant, arranged on the diagonal,
is used in this portable project.*

SIZE
33" × 42"

MATERIALS
Coats & Clark Red Heart Luster Sheen (sport-weight acrylic), 2 oz/180 yd skeins: 5 skeins White (MC); 2 skeins each Pink (A) and Peach (B); 3 skeins Aqua (C)

Size F/5 crochet hook (or size for gauge)

GAUGE
Each square = 3⅛"

SEE
Clusters, Reverse Slip Stitch, and Working in Rounds

NOTE
Joining slip stitch counts as last chain of round.

THE AFGHAN

SQUARE 1 (make 63)
With A, ch 4; join with sl st to form ring.

Rnd 1 (right side): Ch 4 (first tr), [yo 2 times, insert hook in ring, yo, draw up a lp, (yo, draw through 2 lps)—2 times], repeat between [] 1 time more, yo, draw through all 3 lps on hook (**cluster made**), *ch 2, repeat between [] 3 times, yo, draw through all 4 lps on hook, repeat from * 6 times more, ch 1; join with sl st to top of first cluster; end.

Rnd 2: With right side facing, join C in any ch-2 sp; ch 3 (first dc), **don't** turn, 2 dc in sp, ch 2, 3 dc in same sp, ch 1, 3 dc in next sp, (ch 1, 3 dc in next sp, ch 2, 3 dc in same sp, ch 1, 3 dc in next sp) 3 times; join with sl st to top of ch-3; end.

Rnd 3: With right side facing, join MC in any corner sp; work as for Rnd 2, making 1 more 3-dc group per side; end.

SQUARE 2 (make 48)
Work as for Square 1, **but** use B where A is called for.

HALF-SQUARE 3 (make 16)
With B, ch 4; join with sl st to form ring.

Rnd 1: Ch 5 (first tr, ch 1), [yo 2 times, insert hook in ring, yo, draw up a lp, (yo, draw through 2 lps)—2 times], repeat between [] 2 times more, yo, draw through all 4 lps on hook (**cluster made**), *ch 2, repeat between [] 3 times, yo, draw through all 4 lps on hook, repeat from * 2 times more, ch 1, tr in ring; end.

Rnd 2: Join C in first ch-1 sp; ch 4 (first dc, ch 1), **don't** turn, 3 dc in same sp, (ch 1, 3 dc in next sp) 2 times, ch 2, 3 dc in same sp (**corner made**), (ch 1, 3 dc in next sp) 2 times, ch 1, dc in same sp; end.

Rnd 3: Join MC in first ch-1 sp; ch 3 (first dc), **don't** turn, 3 dc in same sp, (ch 1, 3 dc in next sp) 3 times, ch 2, 3 dc in same sp, (ch 1, 3 dc in next sp) 3 times, dc in same sp; end.

BABY FLORAL ASSEMBLY DIAGRAM

Shading indicates diagonal strip orientation.

ASSEMBLY

Refer to Assembly Diagram. With right sides facing, MC, and sl st, catching outer lps only, crochet squares together to form diagonal strips, as indicated by shading on diagram. Join diagonal strips in same manner.

EDGING

With right side facing, join MC at upper left corner-joining.

Rnd 1: Ch 1, *3 sc in corner-joining, 2 sc in each sp and joining across long edge to corner, 3 sc in corner-joining, (sc in each ch-1 sp and dc to point, 3 sc in ch-2 sp at point, sc in each ch-1 sp and dc to V, at V work sc 3 tog over ch-1 sp, joining, and ch-1 sp), repeat between () across short edge to corner, repeat from * 1 time more; join with sl st to first sc.

Rnd 2: Ch 1, **don't** turn, work a reverse sl st in each st of previous rnd; join with sl st to first reverse sl st; end.

Secure and trim loose ends.

Baby Ribbons

Beginner

*Make a pretty ribbon-patterned coverlet
for that special little one! Double crochet and
front-post triple crochet are used in this
quick-to-complete project.*

SIZE
43″ × 43″

MATERIALS
Phildar Leader (worsted-weight acrylic), 3½ oz/216 yd
  balls: 7 balls White (MC); 1 ball each Aqua (A) and
  Peach (B)
Size H/8 crochet hook (or size for gauge)

GAUGE
11 sts = 3″; 12 rows = 5″ (in pattern stitch)

SEE
Changing Color/End of Row, Reverse Slip Stitch, and
Working around Posts

ONE-PIECE AFGHAN

With MC, ch 157.
Row 1: Dc in 4th ch from hook and each ch across—
155 sts.
Row 2: Ch 3 (first dc), turn, sk first st, dc in each st
across.
Row 3: With A, repeat Row 2.

Row 4 (right side): With MC, ch 3 (first dc), turn, sk
first st, *sk next st current row, working in **front** of
previous row, tr **around post** of dc **below** next st, dc
in next st current row, repeat from * across.
Rows 5–6: With MC, repeat Row 2.
Row 7: With B, repeat Row 2.
Rows 8–10: Repeat Rows 4–6.
Repeat Rows 3–10 eleven times more, then Rows 3–
5 one time; end.

EDGING
With right side facing, join MC.
Rnd 1: Work a rnd of sc evenly around entire piece,
making 3 sc at each corner; join with sl st to first sc.
Rnd 2: Ch 2 (first hdc), **don't** turn, sk first st, hdc in
each st around, making 3 hdc at each corner; join with
sl st to top of ch-2.
Rnd 3: Ch 1, **don't** turn, work a reverse sl st in each
st of previous rnd; join with sl st to first reverse sl st;
end.
Secure and trim loose ends.

Butterflies In Flight

Beginner

*Capture the wonder of flight, a child's delight,
with a whimsical flock of butterflies!
Basic and diagonal color-change granny squares are used
in this quick-to-complete, portable project.*

SIZE
44″ × 44″

MATERIALS
Coats & Clark Red Heart Premier (worsted-weight acrylic), 3½ oz/210 yd skeins: 5 skeins White (MC); Coats & Clark Red Heart Classic (worsted-weight acrylic), 3 oz/170 yd skeins: 4 skeins Pastel Varigated (CC)
Size I/9 crochet hook (or size for gauge)

GAUGE
Each 4-round square = 5″

SEE
Changing Color, Reverse Slip Stitch, and Working in Rounds

NOTE
Joining slip stitch counts as last chain of round.

THE AFGHAN

SQUARE A (make 10)
With MC, ch 4; join with sl st to form ring.

Rnd 1 (right side): Ch 3 (first dc), 2 dc in ring, ch 2, 3 dc in ring, ch 1; with **CC** (**don't** end MC), ch 1, 3 dc in ring, ch 2, 3 dc in ring, ch 1; join with sl st to top of ch-3; **don't** end.

Rnd 2: Continuing with CC, ch 1, **turn,** sl st in corner sp just completed, ch 3 (first dc), 2 dc in sp, *ch 1, 3 dc in next sp, ch 2, 3 dc in same sp, ch 1, 3 dc in next sp, ch 1*; with **MC,** ch 1 (**don't** end CC), 3 dc in same sp, repeat between *s; join with sl st to top of ch-3; **don't** end.

Rnd 3: Continuing with MC, ch 1, **turn,** sl st in corner sp just completed, ch 3 (first dc), 2 dc in sp, *(ch 1, 3 dc in next sp) 2 times, ch 2, 3 dc in same sp, repeat between () 2 times more, ch 1*; with **CC** (**don't** end MC), ch 1, 3 dc in same sp, repeat between *s; join with sl st to top of ch 3; **don't** end.

Rnd 4: Continuing with CC, ch 1, **turn,** sl st in corner sp just completed, ch 3 (first dc), 2 dc in sp, *(ch 1, 3 dc in next sp) 3 times, ch 2, 3 dc in same sp, repeat between () 3 times more, ch 1*; with **MC,** ch 1 (end CC), 3 dc in same sp, repeat between *s, join with sl st to top of ch-3; end.

SQUARE B (make 18)
With MC, ch 4; join with sl st to form ring.

Rnd 1 (right side): Ch 3 (first dc), 2 dc in ring, (ch 2, 3 dc in ring) 3 times, ch 1; join with sl st to top of ch-3.

Rnd 2: Ch 3 (first dc), **turn,** 2 dc in sp, ch 2, 3 dc in same sp, (ch 1, 3 dc in next sp, ch 2, 3 dc in same sp) 3 times; join with sl st to top of ch-3.

Rnd 3: Sl st to corner sp, 2 sl st in sp, ch 3 (first dc), **turn,** 2 dc in sp, ch 2, 3 dc in same sp, ch 1, 3 dc in next sp, (ch 1, 3 dc in next sp, ch 2, 3 dc in same sp, ch 1, 3 dc in next sp) 3 times; join with sl st to top of ch-3.

Rnd 4: Work as for Rnd 3, making 1 more 3-dc group per side; end.

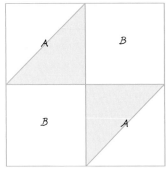

BLOCK 1

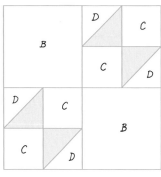

BLOCK 2

Shading indicates areas crocheted with CC.

SQUARE C (make 16)
Work as for Square B **but** end after Rnd 2.

SQUARE D (make 16)
Work as for Square A **but** end after Rnd 2.

BLOCK 1 (make 5)

Assembly
Refer to Block 1 Assembly Diagram. Shading indicates areas crocheted with CC. With right side facing, MC, and sl st, catching outer lps only, crochet squares together. Work edging to complete block.

Edging
With right side facing, join MC in any corner sp.
Rnd 1: Ch 3 (first dc), 2 dc in sp, ch 2, 3 dc in same sp, (ch 1, 3 dc), repeat between () into each sp and joining to corner, *ch 1, 3 dc in corner sp, ch 2, 3 dc in same sp, repeat between () into each sp and joining to corner, repeat from * 2 times more; join with sl st to top of ch-3; end.

BLOCK 2 (make 4)
Work as for Block 1 but use **Block 2 Assembly Diagram.**

AFGHAN ASSEMBLY
Refer to Afghan Assembly Diagram. Crochet blocks together in same manner as for squares.

AFGHAN BORDER
With right side facing, join MC in any corner sp.
Rnd 1: Work Rnd 1 of Block Edging around entire outer edge of afghan; **don't** end.
Rnd 2: Sl st to corner sp, 2 sl st in sp, ch 3 (first dc), **turn,** 2 dc in sp, ch 2, 3 dc in same sp, (ch 1, 3 dc in next sp), repeat between () to corner, *ch 1, 3 dc in corner sp, ch 2, 3 dc in same sp, repeat between () to corner, repeat from * 2 times more; join with sl st to top of ch-3; end.
Rnd 3: With wrong side facing, join CC in any corner sp; work as for Rnd 2, beginning with ch-3; **don't** end.
Rnds 4–10: Repeat Rnd 2; **don't** end.
Rnd 11: Ch 1, **turn,** sc in each st and sp around, making 3 sc in each corner sp; join with sl st to first sc.
Rnd 12: Ch 1, **don't** turn, work a reverse sl st in each st of previous rnd; join with sl st to first reverse sl st; end.
Secure and trim loose ends.

Schoolhouse

Experienced

*Ding, ding . . . hear that bell ring,
calling the country children to school!
Basic and diagonal color-change granny squares
are used in this portable project.*

SIZE
43" × 43"

MATERIALS
Brunswick Windrush (worsted-weight acrylic), 3½ oz/
230 yd skeins: 4 skeins Navy (A); 1 skein each Red
(B), Yellow (C), Aqua (D), Dark Green (E), and
Light Green (F)
Size H/8 crochet hook (or size for gauge)

GAUGE
Each square = 2⅜"

SEE
Changing Color, Reverse Slip Stitch, and Working in
Rounds

NOTE
Joining slip stitch counts as last chain of round.

THE AFGHAN

SOLID-COLOR SQUARE
Ch 4; join with sl st to form ring.
Rnd 1 (right side): Ch 3 (first dc), 2 dc in ring, (ch
2, 3 dc in ring) 3 times, ch 1; join with sl st to top of
ch-3.
Rnd 2: Ch 3 (first dc), **turn,** 2 dc in sp, ch 2, 3 dc in
same sp, (ch 1, 3 dc in next sp, ch 2, 3 dc in same
sp) 3 times; join with sl st to top of ch-3; end.

TWO-COLOR SQUARE
With first color, ch 4; join with sl st to form ring.
Rnd 1 (right side): Ch 3 (first dc), 2 dc in ring, ch 2,
3 dc in ring, ch 1; with **second color** (**don't** end first
color), ch 1, 3 dc in ring, ch 2, 3 dc in ring, ch 1;
join with sl st to top of ch-3; **don't** end.
Rnd 2: Continuing with second color, ch 1, **turn,** sl
st in corner sp just completed, ch 3 (first dc), 2 dc in
sp, *ch 1, 3 dc in next sp, ch 2, 3 dc in same sp, ch
1, 3 dc in next sp, ch 1*; with **first color,** ch 1 (end
second color), 3 dc in same sp, repeat between *s; join
with sl st to top of ch-3; end.

SQUARE 1
Make **11** solid-color squares with A.

SQUARE 2
Make **23** solid-color squares with B.

SQUARE 3
Make **6** solid-color squares with C.

SQUARE 4
Make **14** solid-color squares with D.

SQUARE 5
Make **17** solid-color squares with E.

SQUARE 6
Make **13** solid-color squares with F.

SQUARE 7

Make **2** two-color squares using B for first color and A for second color.

SQUARE 8

Make **2** two-color squares using D for first color and A for second color.

SQUARE 9

Make **2** two-color squares using E for first color and A for second color.

SQUARE 10

Make **5** two-color squares using F for first color and A for second color.

SQUARE 11

Make **4** two-color squares using D for first color and C for second color.

SQUARE 12

Make **4** two-color squares using B for first color and E for second color.

SQUARE 13

Make **10** two-color squares using D for first color and E for second color.

SQUARE 14

Make **8** two-color squares using F for first color and E for second color.

ASSEMBLY

Refer to Assembly Diagram. With right sides facing, corresponding color, and sl st, catching outer lps only, crochet squares together to form vertical strips. Join vertical strips in same manner.

BORDER

With right side facing, join A in any corner sp.

Rnd 1: Ch 3 (first dc), 2 dc in sp, ch 2, 3 dc in same sp, (ch 1, 3 dc), repeat between () into each sp and joining to corner, *ch 1, 3 dc in corner sp, ch 2, 3 dc in same sp, repeat between () into each sp and joining to corner, repeat from * 2 times more; join with sl st to top of ch-3.

Rnds 2–6: Sl st to corner sp, 2 sl st in sp, ch 3 (first dc), **turn**, 2 dc in sp, ch 2, 3 dc in same sp, (ch 1, 3 dc in next sp), repeat between () to corner, *ch 1, 3 dc in corner sp, ch 2, 3 dc in same sp, repeat between () to corner, repeat from * 2 times more; join with sl st to top of ch-3; end after Rnd 6.

Rnd 7: With wrong side facing, join E in any corner sp; work as for Rnd 2, beginning with ch-3; end.

Rnd 8: With right side facing and C, work as for Rnd 7.

Rnd 9: With A, repeat Rnd 7; **don't** end.

Rnd 10: Continuing with A, repeat Rnd 2; end.

Rnd 11: With D, repeat Rnd 7.

Rnd 12: With B, repeat Rnd 8.

Rnd 13: Repeat Rnd 9.

Rnds 14–18: Continuing with A, repeat Rnd 2; **don't** end.

Rnd 19: Ch 1, **turn**, sc in each st and sp around, making 3 sc in each corner sp; join with sl st to first sc.

Rnd 20: Ch 1, **don't** turn, work a reverse sl st in each st of previous rnd; join with sl st to first reverse sl st; end.

Secure and trim loose ends.

SCHOOLHOUSE ASSEMBLY DIAGRAM

4	4	4	4	4	4	4	11	11	4	4
13	4	4	8	8	13	13	11	11	13	13
5	13	13	2	2	5	5	13	13	5	5
5	5	12	7	1	1	1	1	9	5	5
5	12	2	2	7	1	1	1	1	9	5
4	2	2	2	2	2	2	2	2	2	4
13	2	3	3	2	2	3	2	3	2	4
14	2	3	3	2	2	2	12	12	2	6
14	10	1	10	6	6	14	5	5	14	6
10	1	10	6	6	6	14	5	5	14	6
1	10	6	6	6	6	14	5	5	14	6

Two-color square orientation is indicated by diagonal line and color codes in corners.

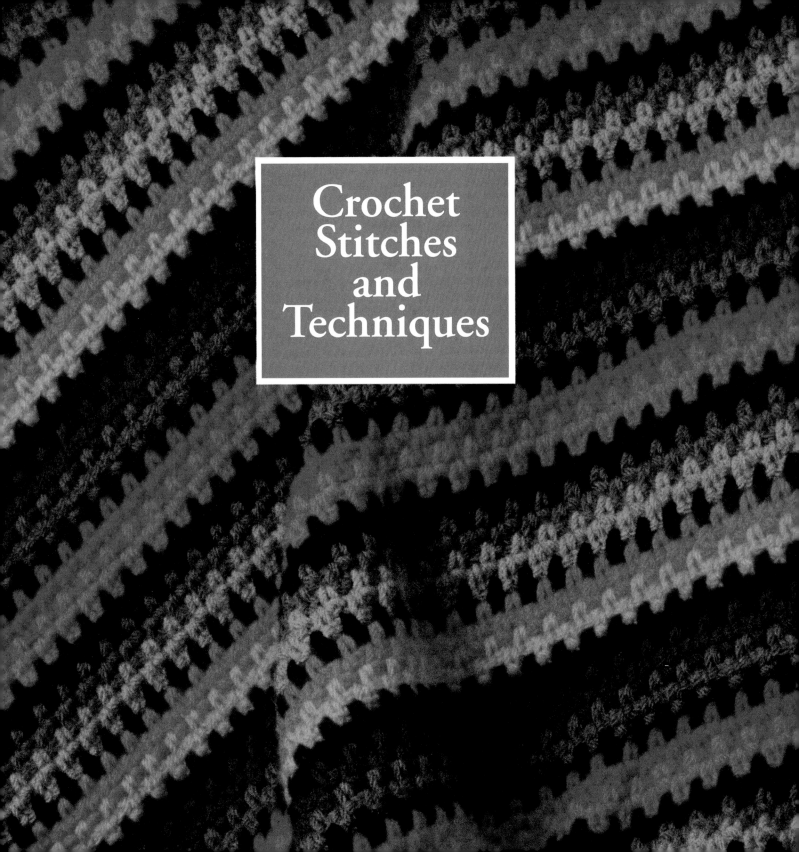

Crochet
Stitches
and
Techniques

Basic Stitches and Techniques

HOLDING THE HOOK AND THE YARN

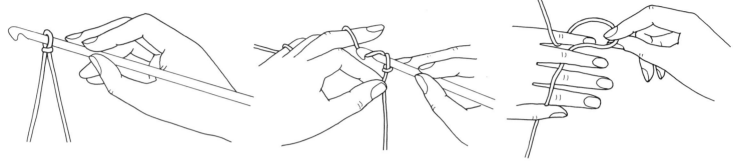

Hold the hook in your right hand, as you would a pencil.

Hold the yarn and the work in your left hand.

Stranding the yarn through the fingers of the left hand, as shown, helps maintain the slight tension necessary for the yarn to flow evenly and freely.

LEFT-HANDED CROCHET

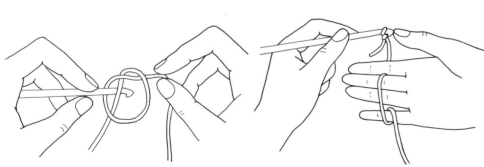

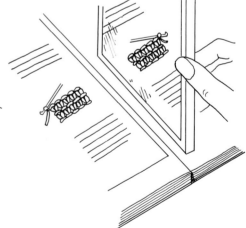

Hold the hook in your left hand.

Hold the yarn and the work in your right hand.

To see how to work a stitch left-handed, hold a mirror beside the illustration. The mirror will reverse the illustration and show how to work the stitch with your left hand.

BASE CHAIN (ch)

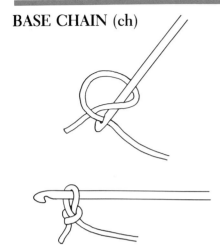

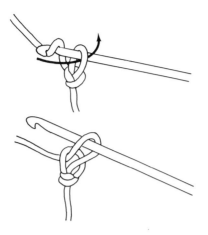

Crochet starts with a base chain. Begin by making a slip knot. Make a loop. Draw the yarn through the loop and tighten.

Wrap the yarn over the hook. Draw the yarn through the loop on the hook to form another loop.

Repeat as many times as required. The loop on the hook is **not** included in the number of chains specified in patterns.

SLIP STITCH (sl st)

Insert the hook into the 2nd chain from hook. Wrap the yarn over the hook. Draw the yarn through **both** the chain and the loop on the hook in one continuous motion—**slip stitch made.**

SINGLE CROCHET (sc)

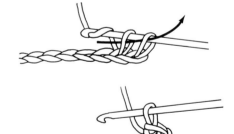

Insert the hook into the 2nd chain from hook. Wrap the yarn over the hook. Draw the yarn through the chain.

Wrap the yarn over the hook again. Draw the yarn through both loops on the hook—**single crochet made.**

HALF DOUBLE CROCHET (hdc)

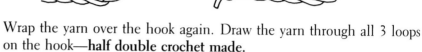

Wrap the yarn over the hook. Insert the hook into the 3rd chain from hook. Draw the yarn through the chain.

Wrap the yarn over the hook again. Draw the yarn through all 3 loops on the hook—**half double crochet made.**

DOUBLE CROCHET (dc)

Wrap the yarn over the hook. Insert the hook into the 4th chain from hook. Draw the yarn through the chain.

Wrap the yarn over the hook again. Draw the yarn through the first 2 loops on the hook.

Wrap the yarn over the hook again. Draw the yarn through both loops remaining on the hook—**double crochet made.**

TRIPLE CROCHET (tr)

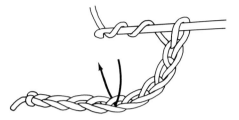  

Wrap the yarn over the hook twice. Insert the hook into the 5th chain from hook. Draw the yarn through the chain.

Wrap the yarn over the hook again. Draw the yarn through the first 2 loops on the hook.

Wrap the yarn over the hook again. Draw the yarn through the next 2 loops on the hook.

Wrap the yarn over the hook again. Draw the yarn through both loops remaining on the hook—**triple crochet made.**

WORKING IN ROUNDS
Make the required number of chains.

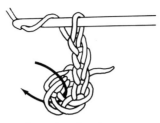

Join with a slip stitch to form a ring by inserting the hook into the first chain and drawing the yarn through both the chain and the loop on the hook.

Then, chain (as for the turning chain when working rows) and work subsequent stitches of the first round into the center of the ring.

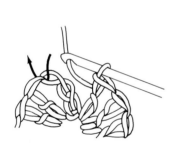

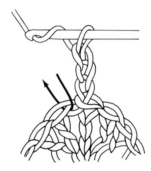

When the round is complete, join with a slip stitch to the top of the starting chain.

Work subsequent rounds into the previous round as directed.

WORKING IN ROWS

The first row is made by working across the base chain as described earlier. Note that 1 or more base chains were skipped at the beginning of the row. These skipped chains resemble the stitch being worked and often count as the first stitch. The number of chains skipped depends on the stitch being used: 1 for single crochet, 2 for half double crochet, 3 for double crochet, and 4 for triple crochet. The number of chains required for the base chain is always greater than the number of stitches in the first row.

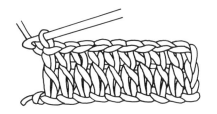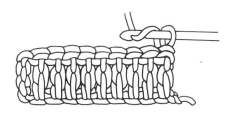

At the end of each row, the work must be turned before the next row can be worked. To turn, 1 or more chains must be made. The number of chains made depends on the stitch being used: 1 for single crochet, 2 for half double crochet, 3 for double crochet, and 4 for triple crochet.

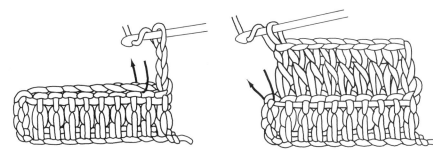

The turning chain often counts as the first stitch of the row. If so, skip the first stitch of the row and work a stitch into the turning chain of the last row when the end of row is reached.

If the turning chain does not count as the first stitch, don't skip the first stitch and don't work into the turning chain of the last row.

Unless otherwise specified, work into both loops at the top of each stitch of the previous row.

WORKING INTO ONE LOOP ONLY

Working into one loop only leaves the unused loop free, creating a ridge.

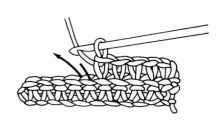 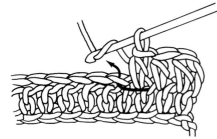

Working into the back loop only creates a ridge on the side of the fabric being worked. The fabric created when working in this manner is more elastic than most crochet stitches, and is frequently used for ribbing.

Working into the front loop only creates a ridge on the opposite side of the fabric.

WORKING AROUND POSTS

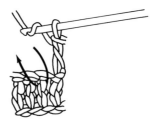 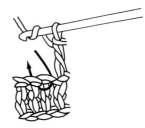

To work a double crochet around the post of a stitch from the **front,** known as a front post double crochet (**fpdc**): Wrap the yarn over the hook, insert the hook from **front to back** into the space between two stitches. Then, bring the hook to the front of the work again, through the space between the second of the stitches and the **next** stitch. Complete the stitch in the usual manner.

To work a double crochet around the post of a stitch from the **back,** known as a back post double crochet (**bpdc**): Wrap the yarn over the hook, insert the hook from **back to front** into the space between two stitches. Then, bring the hook to the back of the work again, through the space between the second of the stitches and the **next** stitch. Complete the stitch in the usual manner.

WORKING WITH CHAIN SPACES

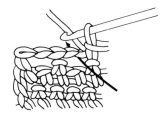

To work **in** a chain space: Insert the hook, from front to back, into the **space** below the chain. Complete the stitch in the usual manner.

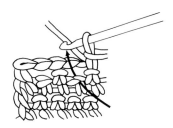

To work **in front** of a chain space: Holding the chain to the **back** of the work, insert the hook, from front to back, into the **skipped stitch** of the **previous row.** Wrap the yarn over the hook; draw up a loop to the height of the current row. Complete the stitch in the usual manner.

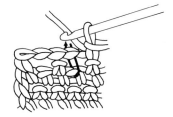

To work **behind** a chain space: Holding the chain to the **front** of the work, insert the hook, from front to back, into the **skipped stitch** of the **previous row.** Wrap the yarn over the hook; draw up a loop to the height of the current row. Complete the stitch in the usual manner.

ENDING

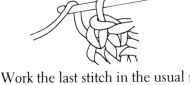

Work the last stitch in the usual manner. Cut the yarn, leaving a sufficient length to secure later (approximately 4"). Wrap the yarn end over the hook. Draw the yarn through the loop remaining on the hook, tightening gently.

JOINING NEW YARN

Always join new yarn at the end of a row. To join new yarn in single, half double, double, or triple crochet (double shown), work in the usual manner until 2 loops remain on the hook. Draw through both loops with the new yarn. Be sure to leave a sufficient length of yarn (approximately 4"), in both the old and the new yarn, to secure later.

CHANGING COLOR

  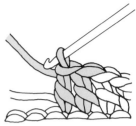

To change color in single, half double, double, or triple crochet (double shown), work in the usual manner until 2 loops remain on the hook. Draw through both loops on the hook with the new color.

When changing color at the end of a row, make the turning chain with the new color.

When changing color within a row, carry the color not in use loosely across the wrong side of the work, and work over it with the new color.

INCREASING (inc)

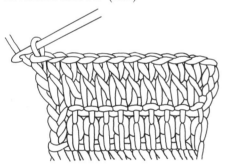

To increase 1 single, half double, double, or triple crochet (double shown), simply work 2 stitches into the same stitch.

156

DECREASING (dec)

Decreases are made by working 2 stitches together.

 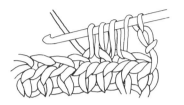 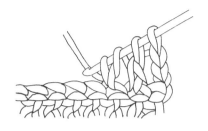

To decrease 1 single crochet within or at the end of a row: Insert the hook into the next stitch; wrap the yarn over the hook; draw a loop through. Repeat into the next stitch; there are 3 loops on the hook. Wrap the yarn over the hook again; draw through all 3 loops on the hook—decrease made.

To decrease 1 single crochet at the beginning of a row: Chain 1, turn, skip the first stitch of the row. Don't work a stitch into the turning chain at the end of the next row.

To decrease 1 half double crochet within or at the end of a row: Wrap the yarn over the hook, insert the hook into the next stitch, wrap the yarn over the hook again, draw a loop through. Repeat into the next stitch; there are 5 loops on the hook. Wrap the yarn over the hook again, draw through all 5 loops on the hook—decrease made.

Work beginning-of-the-row decreases as for single crochet.

To decrease 1 double crochet within or at the end of a row: Wrap the yarn over the hook, insert the hook into the next stitch, wrap the yarn over the hook, draw a loop through, wrap the yarn over the hook again, draw through the first 2 loops on the hook. Repeat into the next stitch; there are 3 loops on the hook. Wrap the yarn over the hook again, draw through all 3 loops on the hook—decrease made.

To decrease 1 double crochet at the beginning of a row: Chain 2, turn, skip the first stitch of the row. Don't work a stitch into the turning chain at the end of the next row.

Special Stitches and Techniques

SURFACE SLIP STITCH

Surface Slip Stitch is used to add color and/or texture to completed crocheted fabrics. The yarn is held at the back of the work throughout. It is important that the stitch tension be neither too tight nor too loose, and that a sufficient length of yarn be left at each end to secure later.

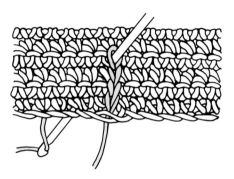

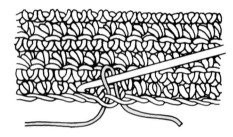

To work a vertical line, begin at the lower edge of the fabric by inserting the hook from **front to back** into the space **between** two stitches. Holding the yarn at the back of the work, wrap the yarn over the hook. Draw the yarn through to the front of the work.

Insert the hook from **front to back** into the space directly above the space just worked. Wrap the yarn over the hook and draw it through to the front of the work **and** through the loop on the hook in one continuous motion. Work subsequent stitches in the same manner.

To work a horizontal line, begin at the edge to your right and work in the same manner, around the posts of stitches, into the spaces between **rows.**

REVERSE SLIP STITCH

Reverse Slip Stitch is used for edging. It is worked from **left to right** into a base row of single crochet.

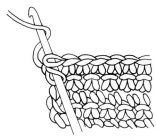
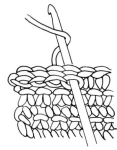

At the end of the single crochet base row, chain 1, but **don't turn.** Keeping the yarn to the left of the work, insert the hook from **front to back** under both loops of the last stitch worked. Wrap the yarn over the hook in a **back to front** direction. Draw the yarn through **both** the stitch and the loop on the hook in one continuous motion.

Insert the hook under the next stitch to **your right.** Wrap the yarn and draw through in the same manner as for the first stitch.

TRIPLE CROCHET BOBBLES

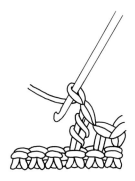

Triple Crochet Bobbles are made on wrong-side rows by working a slip stitch in the stitch before and in the stitch after a triple crochet. This "crumples" the triple crochet, forming a bobble on the right side of the work. These bobbles can be aligned or staggered for an entire fabric, used for a single row, or arranged in a pattern.

CLUSTERS

Clusters are made by working several double crochet stitches together (three shown).

Wrap the yarn over the hook; insert the hook into the chain; wrap the yarn over the hook; draw a loop through; wrap the yarn over the hook again; draw through the first 2 loops on the hook.

Repeat into the **same** chain 2 times more—there are 4 loops on the hook.

Wrap the yarn over the hook again; draw through all 4 loops on the hook—**cluster made.**

SEED PATTERN

Begin by working a row of front loop only single crochet across the wrong side of the fabric. The unused (back) loops are free and form a ridge on the right side of the work.

On the next (right-side) row, work a single crochet into both loops of the first stitch. Skip the next stitch of the current row and work a double crochet into the unused loop of the single crochet one row below.

Work a single crochet into both loops of the next stitch of the current row. Repeat the last two stitches alternately across the fabric.

Repeat the first wrong-side row. To stagger the pattern, work the next right-side row in the same manner as the last right-side row, but begin with a double crochet (rather than a single crochet).

WEAVING

Weaving is used to add color to completed crocheted fabrics. It is important that the stitch tension be neither too tight nor too loose, and that a sufficient length of yarn be left at each end to secure later. Thread a yarn needle with a single strand of yarn.

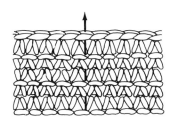

To work a vertical line, begin at the lower edge of the fabric by bringing the needle to the front of the work through the space between two stitches. Draw the yarn through to the front of the work. Insert the needle into the space directly above the space just worked and draw the yarn through to the back of the work. Bring the needle to the front of the work again, through the space directly above the space just worked, and draw the yarn through. Work subsequent stitches in the same manner.

To work a horizontal line, begin at the edge to your right and work in the same manner around the posts of stitches, into the spaces between rows.

FRINGE

Cut a piece of heavy cardboard to half the strand length specified in the directions. For example, if a strand length of 12″ is specified, cut the cardboard to 6″. Then, cut the cardboard to a convenient width (about 8–12″).

Wind the yarn evenly around the cardboard. When the cardboard is full, cut the yarn at one end. Repeat as many times as required.

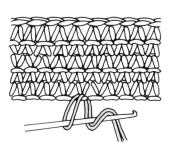

Fold the number of strands specified for each fringe in half. With the wrong side of the work facing and using a crochet hook, draw the folded end through a stitch, forming a loop. Then, draw the loose ends through the loop and tighten.

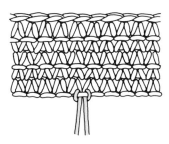

Repeat at the interval specified across the work. Trim the ends to an even length.

CROSS-STITCH EMBROIDERY

Each block on a cross-stitch chart represents 1 single crochet stitch and row. When embroidering, count the single crochet turning chain as 1 stitch. Refer to the chart to be worked, which indicates the color of each stitch.

Thread a yarn needle with a single strand of yarn (approximately armlength). Count over and up to where the first stitch is to be worked.

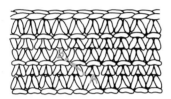 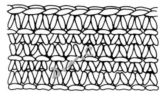 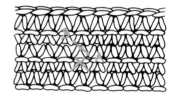

Bring the needle from the back of the work to the front through the space at the lower right-hand corner of the stitch (A), leaving a sufficient length on the wrong side of the work to secure later. Insert the needle through the space at the upper left-hand corner of the stitch (B) and draw the yarn through to the wrong side of the work—tightly enough so the yarn lies flat, but not so tightly that the work puckers.

Bring the needle to the front of the work through the space at the upper right-hand corner of the stitch (C). Insert the needle through the space at the lower left-hand corner of the stitch (D) and draw the yarn through to the wrong side of the work (as previously).

Work each stitch in the same manner, being certain to work from A to B first and from C to D second for every stitch.

Finishing

Use as much care to finish a project as you do to crochet it and you'll be sure to have an afghan you're proud of!

SECURING LOOSE ENDS
Thread the loose end through a tapestry needle. Weave the end through several stitches on the wrong side of the fabric, working several back stitches as you go, to secure it. Don't work too tightly or go through to the right side of the work. Until you feel comfortable with this technique, it's helpful to check the right side of the fabric to make sure that it's still attractive before trimming the end.

BLOCKING
Blocking is seldom necessary since crochet produces a firm fabric. However, if blocking is required, begin by checking the yarn label. If the label says do not iron, or shows the symbol of an iron with an X through it, don't use an iron on the fabric; it could melt! Wet blocking must be done.

If the yarn label indicates that ironing is permitted, pin the piece to the desired shape on a padded surface (such as a thick bath towel). Then, cover the fabric with a pressing cloth and apply a cool iron lightly so as not to flatten the stitches. Let the piece cool before removing it.

To wet-block, pin the piece (with rustproof pins) to the desired shape on a padded surface. Cover with a damp cloth and leave in place until completely dry.

EDGING
Crocheted projects usually require some type of crocheted-edge finishing. To make an attractive edge, stitches must be evenly spaced. There should be sufficient stitches for the edge not to pucker, but not so many that it curls. When a pattern calls for a certain number of stitches to be worked along an edge, this is the number of stitches that will yield an attractive edge.

SEAMS

Begin by pinning the edges of the pieces together, with right sides facing, matching stitches and/or rows. Be particularly careful with stripes.

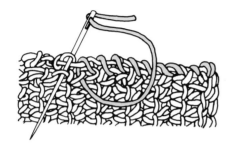

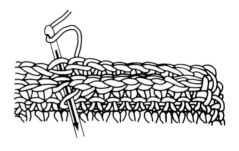

Overcast

This seaming method yields a flat, invisible seam and gives the project a professional finish. Thread a tapestry needle with a length of yarn. Sew the pieces together by inserting the needle under one strand of yarn at the first edge, then over to and under one strand of yarn at the second edge.

Slip Stitch

Use a crochet hook several sizes smaller than the one used to make the fabric and work loosely. Insert the hook through both pieces of fabric. Wrap the yarn over the hook and draw a loop through. Insert the hook through both pieces of fabric again, wrap the yarn over the hook, and draw the yarn through both the fabric and the loop on the hook. Repeat the last step across the fabric.

Index

Yarn Suppliers

For information about retail and mail-order availability of the yarns featured in this book, contact:

Bernat Yarn & Craft Corp.
P.O. Box 387
Uxbridge, MA 01569

Brunswick Yarns
P.O. Box 276
Pickens, SC 29671

Coats & Clark, Inc.
6900 Southpoint Drive North
Jacksonville, FL 32216

Lion Brand Yarn
34 West 15th Street
New York, NY 10001

Patons Yarns
c/o Susan Bates, Inc.
212 Middlesex Avenue
Chester, CT 06412

Phildar USA
6110 Northbelt Parkway
Norcross, GA 30071

William Unger & Co.
P.O. Box 350
Willimantic, CT 06226

Reynolds Yarns
c/o JCA, Inc.
P.O. Box 158
West Townsend, MA 01474

The author would like to thank the yarn suppliers who kindly donated yarn for many of the projects included in the book.

If you would like to order additional copies
of any of our books, call 1-800-678-2803
or check with your local bookstore.